Senior Citizens Abuse in India
And What to Do About It

Siva Prasad Bose and Joy Bose

Published by Joy Bose

Copyright © 2022 Siva Prasad Bose and Joy Bose

All Rights Reserved

Contents

Preface

Acknowledgements

Chapter 1: What is senior citizens abuse

Chapter 2: Problems faced by senior citizens

Chapter 3: Real life examples of senior citizen abuse

Chapter 4: Reasons for senior citizen abuse

Chapter 5: Where to go for help

Chapter 6: Senior citizens protection act

Chapter 7: Senior citizen helplines

Chapter 8: NGOs working with Senior citizens

Chapter 9: Problems in accessing help and strategies to overcome the problems

Chapter 10: Some practical tips

Chapter 11: Conclusion

Appendix A: THE MAINTENANCE AND WELFARE OF PARENTS AND SENIOR CITIZENS ACT, 2007

About the authors

Other Books by Siva Prasad Bose

Preface

Abuse of senior citizens is often an unspoken issue in India. Compared to other kinds of abuse, senior citizen abuse is unique in the fact that it often happens within the same household in which the senior citizens are staying, the abusers are family members on whom the person is dependent and most often the abuses go unreported.

Even though traditionally Indian culture promotes respect for senior citizens, with the changing lifestyles and moving away from joint families and even nuclear families, abuse has become a big issue. Some people may treat their senior citizen parents or family members as a burden and not look after them well, others may be more interested in their property to which they may hold the title, and ill treat them in order to get rights to the property. This problem may have become worse during the recent Covid pandemic, since senior citizens may be less mobile, less familiar with apps and services and also scared to move out for fear of catching the disease.

Moreover, senior citizens are often scared psychologically of courts and police and may be unfamiliar with laws protecting them, in case of abuses. Lack of familiarity with technology is another significant challenge, since many of the protections depend on access to the internet and filing online complaints at various web portals and senior citizen helplines. Because of all this, senior citizens even if they face abuse are reluctant or not able to report it.

Although laws and institutions do exist in India to prevent abuse and provide relief to senior citizens, in practice there may be lack of awareness of such laws, also it may be difficult for senior citizens to access these protections due to reasons mentioned.

This book seeks to address this pervasive issue by presenting real-life examples, exploring the underlying causes, and offering practical solutions to mitigate abuse. By reading this book, you will gain an understanding of the challenges senior citizens face, learn about their legal rights, and discover actionable steps for seeking help and fostering a supportive community.

Through this work, we aim to inspire individuals, families, and policymakers to take collective responsibility in addressing this societal concern.

How to Use This Book

Readers who are currently facing a situation of abuse and need immediate help may turn directly to Chapters 5, 7, and 9, which list helpline numbers, available organizations, and practical strategies for seeking redress. Those who wish to understand the full scope of the problem are encouraged to read the book from beginning to end. Family members and caregivers of senior citizens will find Chapters 4 and 10 particularly relevant. Policymakers and researchers may benefit most from the statistics in Chapter 2 and the legislative framework covered in Chapter 6 and the Appendix.

Acknowledgements

Important Law Books/ References Consulted

• Maintenance and Welfare of Parents and Senior Citizens Act, 2007 (Bare Act) – 2020 by LexisNexis

• Maintenance & Welfare of Parents & Senior Citizens Act, 2007 – 1 January 2015 by Professional Book Publishers

• The Maintenance and Welfare of Parents and Senior Citizens Act, 2007 – 1 January 2019 by Sathpal Puliani (Author, Editor)

• Elder Abuse and Legal Protection by Dr. Harpreet Kaur. Central Law Publications

• Criminal Procedure Code 1973 Volume 1 and 2 by Durga Das Basu. LexisNexis

• Reports by HelpAge India and AgeWell Foundation

Chapter 1: What is senior citizens abuse

Abuse can be defined as cruel or violent treatment of any person that is intended to harm that person, especially when coming from a person who is trusted. When the person being abused by someone (the abuser) is a senior citizen, it can be termed as elderly abuse or senior citizen abuse. It can be one incident of abuse or multiple repeated incidents. It can also manifest as an inaction, such as deliberate neglect of the needs of an elderly person. It can affect both male and female senior citizens.

Globally, the United Nations and World Health Organization have recognized elder abuse as a pressing issue, leading to the establishment of World Elder Abuse Awareness Day on June 15. In India, where a significant percentage of the population is elderly, the issue demands urgent attention.

In this chapter, we look at the various types of abuse which senior citizens might face in India.

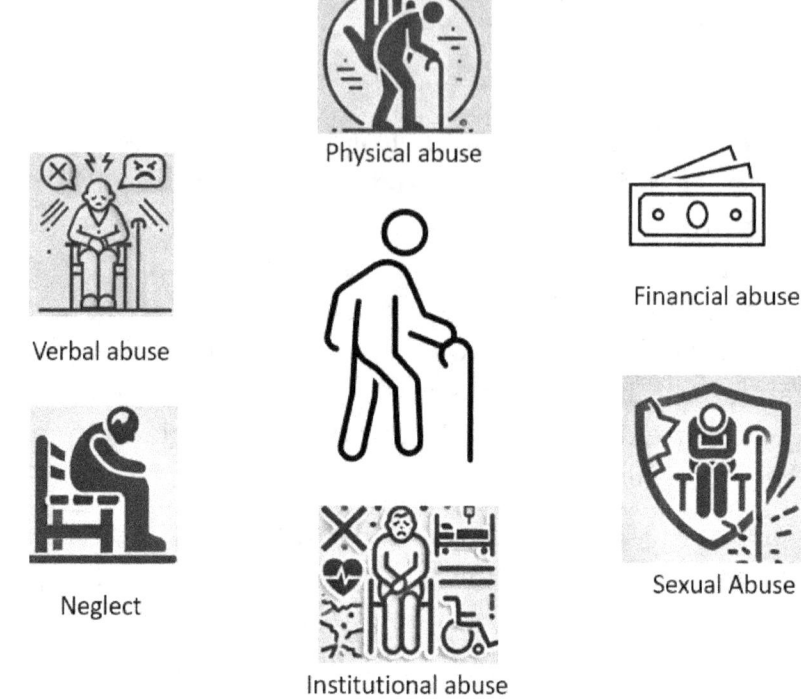

Figure: Different types of senior citizen abuse in India

Figure: Old person lying on a bed. AI generated art by Midjourney AI

1.1 Physical abuse

Physical abuse includes physical violence to the body, such as by beating. It can also include other forms of harm such as depriving someone of food or shelter or medicines, especially if that person was or is dependent on the abuser. It can take forms such as evicting a senior citizen out of the house where they were residing together with the abuser, neglect by not giving medicines or feeding them bad or stale food or not giving them regular meals altogether.

Senior citizens may be physically weak due to old age and may be helpless to fight back at such abuse, especially from close family members with whom they are living and on whom they are dependent for basic necessities.

1.2 Mental, emotional or psychological abuse

Mental abuse includes various forms of mental or psychological harm to the abused person by the abuser, rather than physical violence. This can take forms such as issuing threats, humiliation, insults, verbally abusing the senior citizen, deliberately not listening to their concerns, deliberately doing actions to make their daily life difficult in various cruel ways such as depriving them of basics like water or electricity and so on. It can also take forms like forced confinement or isolation. Emotional abuse can also take the form of emotional blackmail, for example blackmailing the senior citizens to add the abusers as beneficiaries in their will.

The long-term effect of such abuse is to deprive the abused person of their self-esteem and well-being. It can lead to effects such as depression and other mental health issues in the senior citizens subjected to such abuse.

1.3 Neglect and dependency related abuse

Many senior citizens are dependent on their grown children, particularly on their sons and daughters, including daughters in law who are living with them. They may not have fixed incomes since they are no longer able to work as in their youth, even though the property on which they live with their children may be bought from their earnings and be in their name. Hence, the senior citizens may be dependent on others for basics such as food, water, clothing, housing etc. In some cases, the senior citizens might have some income from their pension or provident fund but still might be dependent for other necessities such as food and medical care.

This kind of dependency situation can be used to abuse the senior citizen by depriving them of the things they are dependent on. This can take the form of neglect. Neglect of senior citizens can take different forms, such as not caring for them properly, not providing them proper food and medicines in a timely fashion, not ensuring proper medical treatment as per their needs, not providing proper emotional care or respect, and so on.

1.4 Financial and property related abuse

Financial abuse can take forms such as not supporting the senior citizen financially with respect to their basic needs, stealing the financial or other property of the senior citizens, or forcing them to turn over their property or financial assets to the abuser. This kind of abuse is more common when the perpetrator is a family member or close relative, even the son or daughter, of the persons being abused.

The abusers may feel that the senior citizens are too weak or vulnerable to fight back, so it is a good time to snatch or steal their property by hook or by crook. Or else, the abusers might confine the senior citizens, in whose name the property belongs, to a small room in an isolated section of the property, neglect them, and themselves with their family occupy most of the rooms on the property.

In India, abuse related to property is a common source of abuse for senior citizens, as per multiple surveys by HelpAge India.

Many senior citizens in India even become destitute or homeless, being thrown out of their own house, and are in the streets or slums. They might also face abuse from various sections of society because of their destitution. They may also suffer from forgetfulness or dementia and other psychological problems, which might make their condition even worse due to bad treatment from sections of the society.

Figure: Scene at an old age home. AI generated art by Midjourney AI

1.5 Abuse in old age homes or retirement homes

There are many senior citizens in India who are staying in old age homes. They might have reached there because of a variety of reasons including by their own choice, or being put there by their children who might be unwilling or have no time to take care of them, or because they have been destitute and picked up by some charity organizations or NGOs and put into the old age homes.

Even inside the old age homes, especially in underfunded ones, senior citizens might be subjected to abuse by cruel or unqualified nurses and caregivers. This might even include sexual abuse.

1.6 Digital and Cyber Abuse

A rapidly growing form of abuse targeting senior citizens is digital and cyber fraud. As more services move online, senior citizens who are unfamiliar with technology have become prime targets for sophisticated scams. Unlike physical or emotional abuse which typically involves family members, cyber abuse usually comes from strangers and can cause devastating financial losses in a matter of hours.

1.6.1 Digital Arrest Scams

One of the most alarming scams to emerge in India in recent years is the "digital arrest" fraud. Fraudsters impersonate law enforcement officers — such as CBI, ED, or police — and contact the victim via WhatsApp or video call. They claim the senior citizen is implicated in a serious crime such as drug trafficking or money laundering, and order them to remain on the video call continuously (sometimes for days), isolating them from family. The victim is then coerced into transferring large sums of money to "clear" their name or avoid arrest. In 2024, an 81-year-old victim in Hyderabad lost ₹7.12 crore to such a scam. The Prime Minister of India specifically warned citizens about this scam in his Mann Ki Baat address in October 2024. The key thing to remember: real police will never arrest anyone over a WhatsApp call, nor ask for money to clear your name. If you receive such a call, hang up and contact the cyber crime helpline 1930 immediately.

1.6.2 OTP and KYC Scams

Fraudsters impersonate bank officials or government representatives and call senior citizens claiming their bank account or Aadhaar-linked KYC needs urgent updating. They then extract One-Time Passwords (OTPs) or bank account details and immediately drain the victim's savings. These scams exploit the digital literacy gap and the fear that government services may be disrupted. Senior citizens should be advised never to share OTPs, PINs, or passwords with anyone over phone or message, regardless of who the caller claims to be.

1.6.3 Investment and Deepfake Frauds

Senior citizens with savings are also targeted by fake investment schemes promising high returns, often using WhatsApp groups or fake websites. More recently, deepfake technology has been used to create convincing videos of celebrities or even the victim's own family members endorsing fraudulent schemes. Senior citizens should be advised to consult a trusted family member before making any investment decision, and to verify any video call independently before acting on it.

1.6.4 Legal manipulation through digital means

Another emerging form of abuse is the use of digital platforms to coerce senior citizens into signing gift deeds, property transfers, or power of attorney documents under duress. Sometimes family members may exploit an elderly person's unfamiliarity with digital signatures or online banking to quietly transfer assets. Section 23 of the Maintenance and Welfare of Parents and Senior Citizens Act, 2007 provides that property transfers made under fraud, coercion, or undue influence may be declared void by the Maintenance Tribunal, which offers some protection for victims.

1.7 Conclusion

In this chapter, we have looked at a few types of abuse that senior citizens might face in India. In the following chapters, we go through some of these in more detail, following which we will focus on some remedies.

Chapter 2: Problems faced by senior citizens

In this chapter we study some data related to abuse of senior citizens, to throw some light on the extent and scale of the problem in India.

Senior citizens constitute approximately 8% of India's population of over a billion. Out of this, more than 135 million people (and growing) are elderly senior citizens above 80 years of age. The average life expectancy in India is steadily increasing, leading to an increased number of senior citizens, but lack of corresponding increase of government support.

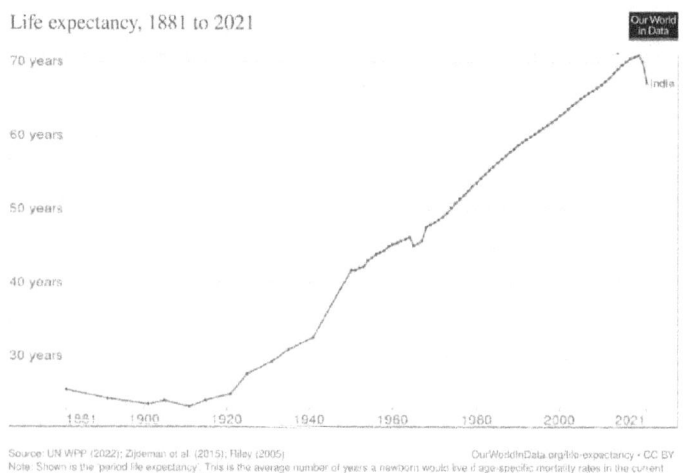

Figure: Life expectancy in India. By Max Roser - Our World in Data: https://ourworldindata.org/grapher/life-expectancy?country=~IND, CC BY-SA 3.0, https://commons.wikimedia.org/w/index.php?curid=115278586

There have been a few studies and surveys on the problems of senior citizens in India related to abuse. They are listed in the following subsections. The references for the data are provided at the end of the chapter.

2.1 Senior citizens abuse within the family

In an article in Press Trust of India, based on a study by AgeWell Foundation, it was reported that about 71% of the senior citizens have been harassed or humiliated by their own family members and relatives. Another 2014 survey by HelpAge found that 50% of the elderly reported experiencing some form of abuse, out of which 77% lived with their families. The HelpAge survey found that 73% of Indian youth also admit that abuse of seniors exists.

However, in most of the cases, the abused senior citizens rarely report the abuse, mostly out of factors such as ignorance of the process or law, or unwillingness to bring disrepute to their family, along with fear of reprisals. Also, since they may be living with and dependent on the abusers, there is a possibility of the abuse becoming worse if they complain about it to others.

Another study by HelpAge India, highlighted in an article in the Hindu newspaper, found that daughters in law abuse the elderly most (44%), followed by their own daughters (32%) and then their sons (24%). One of the reasons for this could be that many daughters in law might be housewives who spend a lot of time during the day with the elderly in the family, while their husbands may be out working. The same study also found that only 24% of the abused senior citizens were willing to report the abuse.

Figure: Figure as per the Hindu article on responsible person, among family members, for abusing senior citizens

2.2 High cost of medical treatment

Government hospitals in India are often poorly equipped, so many senior citizens prefer to go to private hospitals. However, the cost of treatment in such private hospitals is very expensive. For example, there were reports of ICU beds of Covid patients in 2020 being charged at Rupees 80000 per day, 9 lakhs for ICU with ventilator treatment for 10 days in some private hospitals in the big cities. Therefore, one must go for health insurance to help pay the cost of such treatment. The annual rate of medical inflation in India is 14%, among the highest in the world.

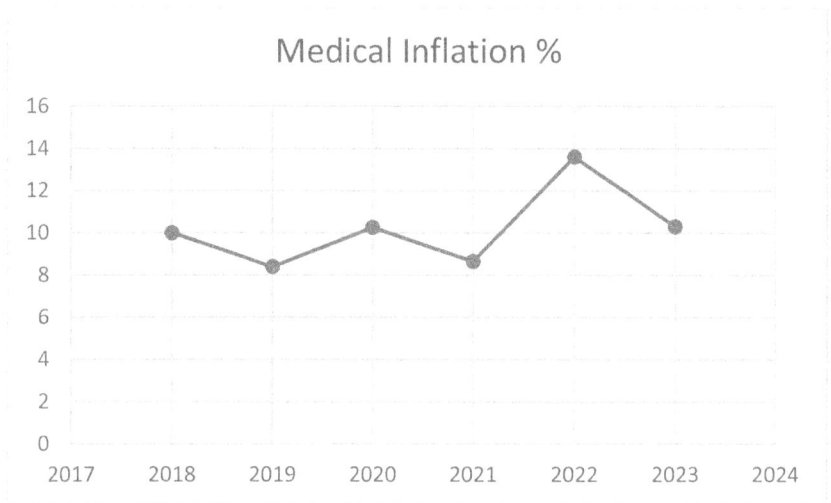

Figure: Medical Inflation in India 2018-2023. Based on Statista report https://www.statista.com/statistics/1466124/india-average-medical-inflation/

Private health insurance in India is primarily targeted at younger individuals. Private health insurance for senior citizens above 65 is often unaffordable, with premiums running into Rs 20000 per year or more, which was the rate around 2020 and could go even higher is subsequent years. This high medical insurance premium results in many senior citizens not having adequate health cover. Even for those senior citizens whose children are working in the corporate sector, many private companies do not cover the medical insurance for parents, they only cover their wife and kids. Also, even if one has corporate insurance cover for their parents and they leave the company or is fired, the medical insurance coverage for their parents from the employer may be cut off suddenly. Another problem is insurance providers suddenly hiking the insurance premiums after a few years.

Also, government health insurance schemes such as Ayushman Bharat often leave out most middle-class people including senior citizens. They are focused on the poorest sections of society and many middle class senior citizens may be not wealthy enough to afford private insurance, yet might not meet the stringent criteria of the government schemes.

2.3 Poverty and homelessness in senior citizens

Millions of elderly people in India are living below the poverty line and have no income security, found a report published by the AgeWell foundation.

Similarly, many of the senior citizens in India are homeless, since they are abandoned by their children. A few lucky senior citizens, having enough money to pay for it, languish in old age homes.

2.4 Problems related to property disputes

Many senior citizens might have property in their name, bought during their working life with their earnings. However, they may have grown up children who are living with them and taking care of the property, and who are desirous of getting complete ownership of the property from their parents as soon as possible. The same holds for other relatives in the extended family, who may perceive the senior citizens as weak and as soft targets, from whom it would be relatively easy to snatch the property.

In a survey, it was reported that about 48% of senior citizens in India were trapped in one or more property related disputes, including revoking of their will. The same survey showed that 58 per cent petitioners faced physical abuse (beating and hitting), 28 per cent suffered mental torture.

In another survey reported in the Hindu newspaper, it was reported that 57% of calls to the Elders helpline number in Bangalore were related to intra familial issues including property disputes.

2.5 Isolation due to Covid lockdown

In another survey published in Times of India newspaper, 71% of senior citizens said their abuse had increased due to the ongoing Covid pandemic and its subsequent lockdown. During the pandemic, many senior citizens were more reluctant to get out of the house for fear of catching Covid and being a more vulnerable group for the disease. This would lead to lack of physical activity, increased isolation, bringing with it an increased amount of domestic abuse and all kinds of mental health related problems.

2.6 Lack of access to technology

Many senior citizens, especially from the middle class or lower middle class and those who are in small cities, might be unfamiliar with technology including digital payments. Part of the reasons for this would be that smartphones and digital payment apps have only developed recently and were not there say 20 years ago. Similarly, some senior citizens might be old fashioned and prefer to shop their groceries from small and personal kinara stores as opposed to the modern malls.

For such people, increased modernization and digitalization might cause more problems and inconvenience. They might be unable to use digital services like Uber and digital money transfers like Paytm. They may not even know how to use ATMs and credit cards, and prefer cash and cheque transactions.

All these problems may be even worse in case of female senior citizens especially those who are housewives, as their interaction with the wider society is further limited.

2.7 Lack of empathy from various service providers

Lack of empathy, understanding and patience from various service providers in India can also be a contributing factor to increasing the problems of senior citizens. In places like supermarkets, ticket booking offices, banks or government offices, the employees may not have been provided training specifically to be senior citizen friendly. This can lead to lack of understanding from such employees who are already stressed and pressed for time, leading to difficulties when senior citizens try to access their services. The senior citizens may be suffering from conditions such as forgetfulness or being unable to articulate their requirements precisely, leading to further difficulties while accessing the services.

The same holds for institutions meant for protection of senior citizens, such as police and judiciary. The senior citizens may find it difficult to raise their complaints against abuse or to seek relief from the police or courts. The reasons can be the slow moving, bureaucratized and sometimes corrupt judiciary, police and other institutions. In some cases, they may not know of the procedures for lodging complaints, which often change without notice or might require online e-filing, and hence might be ignored or ill-treated by these institutions. The problem can be even worse if their abusers turn out to have political or other connections.

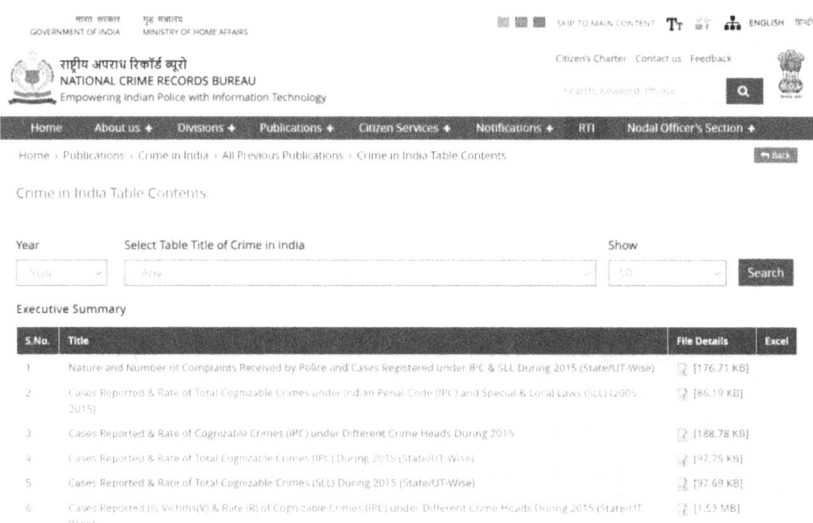

Figure: Crimes report at the National Crime Records Bureau (NCRB) website

2.8 Crimes report by National Crimes Records Bureau (NCRB)

National Crimes Records Bureau or NCRB is the Indian government agency responsible for collecting and compiling statistics on all kinds of crimes reported to the police. They file annual reports containing breakdown of crimes under different categories. Since senior citizens are usually reluctant to approach the police, the crime statistics against senior citizens suffers from underreporting. The statistics mostly include financial and other crimes by strangers such as dacoity, robbery and murder, and ignore the crimes committed by persons within the same household, which are the most common form of senior citizens abuse but are very difficult to report. Still, the report does highlight a number of crimes where the victims were elderly people.

2.9 Updated Statistics: 2023–2024

Since earlier sections of this chapter were written, several updated surveys and reports have provided a clearer picture of senior citizen abuse in India. The following findings reflect the situation as of 2024.

The 2024 HelpAge India report on ageing found that approximately 7% of elders openly admitted to experiencing abuse, with the figure rising to 11% among lower socio-economic groups. Sons (42%) and daughters-in-law (28%) remain the top perpetrators. Significantly, 94% of abused elders were found to have at least one chronic disease, and abuse was found to be strongly correlated with illiteracy and annual household income below ₹1 lakh. A 2023 HelpAge women-focused survey found that 16% of older women had faced abuse, of which 50% was physical and 46% emotional or disrespect-related.

The NCRB 2023 Crime in India report recorded 27,886 cases of crimes against senior citizens, a slight decrease from 28,545 in 2022. The top categories were simple hurt

(27.3%), theft (14.8%), and forgery, cheating, and fraud (12.5%). Maharashtra, Madhya Pradesh, and Tamil Nadu reported the highest number of cases. As with previous years, these figures significantly undercount intra-family abuse, which rarely gets reported to police.

A major new dimension highlighted in recent surveys is the digital divide. Approximately 59% of Indian senior citizens lack access to smartphones or digital services, making them more vulnerable to isolation, scams, and exclusion from online government schemes. This gap is particularly pronounced in rural areas and among women senior citizens.

On a more positive note, the Government of India expanded the Ayushman Bharat Pradhan Mantri Jan Arogya Yojana (AB-PMJAY) in 2024 to cover all senior citizens aged 70 and above with free health insurance of up to ₹5 lakh per year, irrespective of income. This directly addresses the high medical cost burden discussed in Section 2.2 and covers approximately 6 crore senior citizens. Eligible seniors can apply for their Ayushman card through the AB-PMJAY portal, a Common Service Centre, or by calling 14567.

2.10 Urban vs Rural Differences in Senior Citizen Abuse

The nature of senior citizen abuse in India differs significantly between urban and rural settings. In urban areas, the predominant forms are property disputes and financial abuse, isolation due to nuclear family living arrangements, and increasingly, digital and cyber fraud. Urban senior citizens often have more awareness of their legal rights and access to helplines, but may face greater social isolation as joint family structures have largely broken down.

In rural areas, abuse more commonly takes the form of neglect driven by poverty, physical abuse linked to property inheritance disputes, and the stranding of elderly parents when adult children migrate to cities for work. Rural senior citizens typically have less awareness of legal protections and face greater difficulty accessing tribunals, NGOs, and helplines. The absence of a local senior citizen cell or functioning 14567 access point is more likely in rural settings. At the same time, rural areas with stronger community and social ties may provide some informal protection through community pressure and social norms.

Understanding these differences matters for both policy and practice. Awareness campaigns, helpline availability, and legal literacy programs need to be specifically tailored for rural populations rather than assuming a one-size-fits-all approach.

2.11 The Gender Dimension: Women Senior Citizens at Higher Risk

Senior citizen women face a significantly higher risk of abuse than men. The 2023 HelpAge India women-focused survey found that 16% of older women experienced abuse, compared to a lower overall average. Among abused older women, 50% experienced physical abuse and 46% faced disrespect or emotional abuse. Widows are particularly vulnerable: upon the death of their husband, they may face pressure from sons or other relatives to surrender property rights, are more likely to be isolated socially, and often have less familiarity with legal processes and technology.

Women senior citizens who have spent their lives as homemakers are also more dependent on family members for financial support and mobility, making it harder to leave abusive situations or seek outside help. Illiteracy — more common among older women in India — further compounds this vulnerability. The National Commission for Women (Section 5.5) can be specifically approached by women senior citizens in addition to the general senior citizen resources listed in this chapter.

2.12 Conclusion

In this chapter, we went into more detail with statistics of different problems faced by the senior citizens, obtained from different research reports and newspaper articles.

References:

- Annual report 2017-18, AgeWell Foundation, http://www.agewellfoundation.org/wp-content/uploads/2018/07/Annual_Report-2017-18.pdf
- Agewell Foundation, 2014, Human Rights of Older People in India: A reality check. https://social.un.org/ageing-working-group/documents/fifth/AgewellFoundationHumanRightsofOlderPeopleinIndia.pdf
- Press Trust of India, June 2019. Over 71 pc senior citizens in India victims of abuse by family

- members: Survey. https://economictimes.indiatimes.com/news/politics-and-nation/over-71-pc-senior-citizens-in-india-victims-of-abuse-by-family-members-survey/articleshow/69777963.cms?from=mdr
- Hindu, June 2013. Daughters-in-law abuse elderly more, says HelpAge India study. https://www.thehindu.com/news/cities/Thiruvananthapuram/daughtersinlaw-abuse-elderly-more-says-helpage-india-study/article4817075.ece
- PTI, Jan 2018. 48 per cent senior citizens involved in property-related disputes: Survey. https://housing.com/news/48-per-cent-senior-citizens-involved-property-related-disputes-survey/
- Hindustan Times, Jul 2018. Abuse of elderly for property: A house divided by greed. https://www.hindustantimes.com/punjab/abuse-of-elderly-for-property-a-house-divided-by-greed/story-vwLYHVC6bZqNYjWrsdNBFI.html
- The Hindu, June 2014. Intra-familial elder abuse attributed to property disputes. https://www.thehindu.com/news/cities/bangalore/intrafamilial-elder-abuse-attributed-to-property-disputes/article6115215.ece
- Times of India, June 2020. Abuse has increased during lockdown, say 71 percent of elderly. https://timesofindia.indiatimes.com/india/abuse-has-increased-during-lockdown-say-71-of-elderly/articleshow/76377324.cms
- IANS and Financial Express, June 2017. As India ages, over 61% of elderly will have no income

- security by 2050 https://www.financialexpress.com/economy/as-india-ages-over-61-of-elderly-will-have-no-income-security-by-2050/717511/
- Economic Times, Nov 2019. Are independent health insurance covers for seniors unaffordable? Here's what experts say. https://economictimes.indiatimes.com/wealth/insure/health-insurance/are-independent-health-insurance-covers-for-seniors-unaffordable-heres-what-experts-say/articleshow/71982283.cms?from=mdr
- World Health Organization, Elder Abuse in India, country Report. https://www.who.int/ageing/projects/elder_abuse/alc_ea_ind.pdf?ua=1
- NCRB, Crime in India 2019 report. Website: https://ncrb.gov.in/en/crime-india-2019-0
- Volume 2 of the 2019 NCRB report contains a breakdown of crimes against senior citizens: https://ncrb.gov.in/sites/default/files/CII%202019%20Volume%202.pdf
- NCRB, Crimes against senior citizens, 2015 report https://ncrb.gov.in/sites/default/files/crime_in_india_table_additional_table_chapter_reports/Chapter%2020-15.11.16_2015.pdf
- Helpage India. National Survey: A youth perspective on elder abuse. 2015. https://www.helpageindia.org/wp-content/themes/helpageindia/pdf/Elder-Abuse-The%20Indian-Youth-Speaks-Out.pdf

- Rajat Banerjee. Rising Cases of Elder Abuse in India. Economic and Political Weekly. Vol. 58, Issue No. 35, 02 Sep, 2023. Published on 20 January 2024. https://www.epw.in/journal/2023/35/letters/rising-cases-elder-abuse-india.html
- Deepika Chelani. Medical inflation in India reaches alarming rate of 14%, reveals report
- . Mint, 22 Nov 2023. https://www.livemint.com/money/personal-finance/medical-inflation-in-india-reaches-alarming-rate-of-14-reveals-report-11700634947658.html

Chapter 3: Real life examples of senior citizen abuse

In this chapter, we go through a few real-life examples to give an idea of how senior citizen abuse is prevalent in our society.

3.1 Newspaper clippings

Below are some extracts from recent newspaper clippings.

3.1.1 Example where video is shared of a senior citizen being severely abused by her own son

The New Indian Express, 30 December 2020: Man arrested after video of him brutally torturing mother goes viral

THIRUVANANTHAPURAM: After the back-to-back videos from Neyyattinkara where a couple had accidentally set themselves ablaze over a land dispute, a new video has emerged from Kerala that's shocked the conscience of the public. Sitting on the floor and leaning against the wall, Shahida, a woman in her late fifties, is taking blows on her face. Her shrieks and loud prayers notwithstanding, the attacker keeps on slapping her and throwing kicks on her face and ribs. A feeble female voice can be heard uttering something which suggests "I am not going to interfere." Apparently, it's this woman, who is shooting the video. As the video went viral, Ayiroor police registered a suo motu case and arrested Razaq. The police said the incident happened a month back and the victim had then refused to lodge a complaint. Razaq was working as a private bus cleaner and is said to be a drug addict.

3.1.2 Example where a senior citizen was evicted out of her house by her sons over property

Mirror Now Digital. Dec 6 2020. Humanity evicted: 99-year-old mother thrown out of house after being physically, mentally tortured by 4 sons

Bhopal: A 99-year-old mother was allegedly forced to spend two days on the road two months ago after her four sons threw out of the house in Madhya Pradesh. The incident came to fore after the elderly woman, an Ashok Nagar city resident, moved the Bhopal district court last week, seeking Rs 10,000 as monthly maintenance allowance from her sons and a right to live respectfully until death.

Elderly woman alleges torture by sons: The nonagenarian stated that she had six sons of whom the eldest died, while the youngest is differently-abled. She had been staying with the other four sons – two are government servants and two make a living from farming – since her husband's death in 2001. "After the death of my husband in 2001, my four sons encroached upon the whole property, including an 8-acre agricultural land and a house in Ashok Nagar. They cursed and harassed me. They starved me. I have been tortured physically and mentally for the past few years," a report by Hindustan Times quoted the elderly mother as saying.

3.1.3 Example where a senior citizen couple were beaten up by neighbors over a property dispute

Mumbai Mirror, Sep 19, 2016. Wadala elderly couple beaten up by neighbor

Refusal to sell their flat prompted assault, alleges couple; accused counters with assault complaint of his own

Mumbai: A fight between two neighbors in Wadala took an ugly turn when two senior citizens were beaten up with hockey sticks at their residence in Kidwai Colony and ended up with fractures and stitches. Haroon Siddiqui, 75, and Zarina Siddiqui, 68, were rushed to KEM Hospital where Haroon received five stitches and is being treated for four fractures while Zarina received 15 stitches. Police sources said that the two families have been locked in a dispute over the Siddiqui's ground-floor apartment for more than two years now as the Khan family – accused by the Siddiquis of attacking them – has been wanting to purchase it despite Zarina and Haroon's refusal.

3.1.4 Example where a senior citizen was beaten up by son and daughter in law for demanding maintenance amount

Sambad. Oct 14, 2019: Beaten Up By Son, Daughter-In-Law, Elderly Woman Seeks Police Help

Phulbani: The value of maternal love seems to have declined with domination of money for which old age appears to be a curse for many in modern society. Here's a heart-rending incident reported from Phulbani town of Kandhamal district where a 70-year-old woman was

beaten up by her son and daughter-in-law over a sum of money. Being tortured and humiliated by children, the victim approached police seeking justice at old age. According to reports, the elderly couple Utsab Nayak and Kuntala Nayak of Amalapada area has three sons and one daughter. However, they are staying with daughter as their sons expressed disinterest to keep parents with them. As part of their responsibility towards parents, the sons were paying some money to them every month.

Sources said that the second son Ramesh Nayak of the couple had not paid his part of money in past two months for which Kuntala had visited his home to know the reason. When she asked his son for money, the latter along with his wife started assaulting her physically in front of home. Later, the duo dragged the old woman into the house and beat her up without mercy for demanding money.

3.2 Examples from reports

Below are some extracts from reports by Agewell and HelpAge India.

3.2.1 Extracts from a report on Elder Abuse by HelpAge India

HelpAge India. Elder Abuse in India 2014 Chapter 4, Personal Experience of Abuse:

Across the cities, 50% of the elders admitted to having personally experienced abuse, though 83% of all elders surveyed, are of the view that it is prevalent in society. Across the cities, Verbal Abuse (41 %), Disrespect (33%) and Neglect (29%) were the major types of abuse faced by the elderly. Elders across cities were asked about the abusers within their family. The Daughter-in-law (61%) and Son (59%) emerged as the topmost perpetrators. This is a trend that is continuing from the previous years. Not surprisingly, 77% of those surveyed, live with their families. Across the cities, 'Emotional dependence on the abuser' (46%) and 'Economic dependence on the abuser' (45%) are the major reasons for them being abused. Among those who experienced abuse, 41% did not report the abuse to anyone. The elderly who were abused, but, did not report were asked about the reasons for the same. The majority stated that they wanted "To maintain confidentiality of family matter" (59%). 17 %"Did not know how to deal with the problem." The highest awareness of a Redressal Mechanism is the Police Helplines at 64%, 14% are aware of the Maintenance Act and 9% are even aware of the HelpAge India Elder Helplines. However, 18% are not aware of any mechanism.*

HelpAge India. Elder Abuse in India 2014 Chapter 5. Beaten in body, mind and spirit. The dark stories of Elder Abuse in India

From Bengaluru: economic exploitation by Abuser "They want my money and so they abuse me"

Ramaiah (name changed), is a 67 year old from ITI Colony in Bengaluru. He has a rental income which is good enough to take care of his and his wife's needs. However, his son and daughter in law want this money for themselves and constantly abuse the couple over it. Ramiah's deteriorating

health and the resultant medical expenses force him to keep the money to meet this need. This caused many a friction between him and his son and daughter in law so much so that the he and wife chose to live separately and face life by themselves. His relatives were no help in resolving the issue as they merely laughed at Ramaiah's family problems. Today, he finds solace in the fact that his wife is by his side.

3.2.2 Extracts from a report on Human Rights of Elderly in India by AgeWell Foundation

Agewell Foundation. Human Rights of the Elderly in India: a Critical Reflection on Social Development. July 2015

In all, 2/3rd respondents i.e. 65.2% elderly respondents claimed that older persons face neglect in old age. More than half (54.1%) respondents said that older persons suffer elder abuse in their families/society. Every third elderly claimed that elderly face domestic violence (physical/verbal) in old age. Every fourth elderly, i.e. 25.3% elderly admit that older persons are being exploited by their family members. In all, 89.7% respondents out of 2705 respondents facing elder abuse reportedly said that elderly face mistreatment in old age mostly due to financial reasons. In all, 96.4% of elderly abused respondents claimed that they face mistreatment due to emotional factors. In all, 67.5% of elderly abused respondents said that they face physical elder abuse in general. According to 25% elderly respondents younger generations consider elderly family members as burden on their family. Equal number of elderly (25%) said that generation gap is the main reason behind violation of human rights of older persons In all, 20% elderly respondents admit that their younger family members are unable to take care of their elderly family members.

References

- The New Indian Express, 30 December 2020: Man arrested after video of him brutally torturing mother goes viral
- Mirror Now Digital. Dec 6 2020. Humanity evicted: 99-year-old mother thrown out of house after being physically, mentally tortured by 4 sons
- Mumbai Mirror, Sep 19, 2016. Wadala elderly couple beaten up by neighbor
- Sambad. Oct 14, 2019: Beaten Up By Son, Daughter-In-Law, Elderly Woman Seeks Police Help
- HelpAge India. Elder Abuse in India 2014 Report. 2014
- Agewell Foundation. Human Rights of the Elderly in India: a Critical Reflection on Social Development. July 2015
- https://www.helpageindia.org/wp-content/themes/helpageindia/pdf/elderabuseindia14.pdf
- https://www.agewellfoundation.org/pdf/reports/Human%20Rights%20of%20Elderly%20in%20India%20-%20A%20Critical%20Reflection%20on%20Social%20Development%20-%20July%202015.pdf

Chapter 4: Reasons for senior citizen abuse

Having seen the statistics related to the problem of senior citizen abuse in the previous chapters, in this chapter we go through some of the possible reasons behind this abuse, and why senior citizens are more vulnerable.

4.1 Economic reasons for elder abuse

With the changing society and widespread unemployment in India especially during the Covid-19 pandemic, coupled with rising inflation, many young people may not have the means to take care of their senior citizen relatives in India. The high costs of medical insurance and treatment further add to the problem of making senior citizens feel like a burden to young people.

4.2 Lack of a comprehensive social welfare system

Unlike developed countries such as European countries, India has a very small or non-existent welfare system for senior citizens. Therefore, government help is very less and difficult to find, especially for middle class senior citizen people who might be earning a little more than the threshold for getting access to schemes of the government meant primarily for the economically weaker sections.

4.3 Reasons with married children

Married people may feel that they have their own family to support, so they have no time or energy to bother with taking care of their old parents. Sometimes they might face pressure from the wider society and from their wives (in case of working men) to dedicate their salary and resources to their own family and not to their parents, and also to live separately from their parents.

4.4 Changing lifestyles in cities

In the west, it is typical for young people to leave their parents' homes at 16 and move out, there is also no tradition of taking care of parents in their old age.

Indians sometimes tend to ape the west and Western society, disregarding our traditional respect for old people. Hence, this idea of the children moving out of the house or trying to be independent and cut off from their parents is becoming a common trend in India too, especially with the increased pace of modernization.

4.5 Children who are working migrants

With the advent of modern lifestyles, the joint families of the past, which used to act like welfare systems for elders in the joint family, have all but disappeared. Many times, the husband and wife with their kids have to move to a different city to work, which is far away from the native place where their senior citizen parents live.

Such problems of senior citizen mistreatment and abuse are common with all levels of Indian society: with the middle-class white-collar IT workers who are working in IT firms in

IT hub cities like Bangalore or Gurgaon as well as migrant laborers.

4.6 Lack of awareness in society and media

Mass media such as TV and newspapers rarely focus on the problems of senior citizens. They may even show them in a negative light, such as in soap operas and films. The old people are often portrayed as being regressive, with outdated values that are not compatible with modern society, being ignorant or forgetful, unable to use technology, often portrayed as villains, etc. Often, mothers in law are shown in bad light in soap operas and films in India.

4.7 Domestic Disputes

Sometimes domestic disputes, such as between the daughters in law and senior citizen parents, can also become a cause of abuse. Sometimes, the husband and wife cannot get along, or else the mother-in-law and daughter in law cannot get along. Often in such cases, the men start living separately or else there is neglect and abuse of the old parents in law. The HelpAge study in the Hindu article mentioned in the previous chapter found that daughters in law abused the elderly in 44% of the cases. The root causes of this could be changing cultures, inter generation gap, and other social issues in India.

4.8 Digital Illiteracy and Cyber Vulnerability

As discussed in Chapter 1, the rapid growth of digital financial fraud targeting senior citizens has emerged as a significant new cause and form of abuse. Senior citizens who are unfamiliar with smartphones, online banking, and digital communication are especially vulnerable to scammers who impersonate government officials, bank employees, or even family members. The psychological tactics used in "digital arrest" scams — isolation, fear, urgency, and impersonation of authority — closely mirror the dynamics of emotional and financial abuse within families, but are carried out by strangers at scale.

The structural reasons for this vulnerability include: the rapid pace of digitization of financial and government services, insufficient digital literacy programs targeting older populations, the social isolation of many senior citizens which makes it harder to consult trusted family members before acting, and the low awareness of cybercrime reporting mechanisms such as the national cyber helpline 1930. Making senior citizens aware of these vulnerabilities and providing simple, practical digital safety guidance — as discussed in Chapter 10 — is therefore an important step in prevention.

4.9 Caregiver Burnout

Not all abuse of senior citizens stems from malice or greed. A significant and often overlooked cause is caregiver burnout — the physical, emotional, and financial exhaustion experienced by family members who are providing ongoing care for an elderly relative. As India's elderly population grows and chronic illnesses become more prevalent, many adult children find themselves providing intensive care without adequate support, training, or respite.

Caregiver burnout can manifest as irritability, verbal outbursts, or neglectful behaviour that the caregiver themselves may not recognize as abusive. Contributing factors include: providing care without sufficient help from other family members, managing a full-time job alongside caregiving responsibilities, the financial strain of paying for medicines and medical treatment, lack of awareness of government schemes or community support, and the emotional difficulty of watching a parent's health decline. In some cases, a caregiver who was themselves raised in an abusive household may unknowingly repeat those patterns.

Recognising caregiver burnout as a legitimate issue does not excuse the resulting abuse — senior citizens still deserve protection regardless of the cause. However, addressing the root causes of caregiver stress through better government support, respite care options, and mental health resources for caregivers is an important part of any long-term strategy to reduce elder abuse. Family members who are struggling should seek support from NGOs like HelpAge India or call 14567, which can also provide guidance to caregivers, not just to those being abused.

4.10 Conclusion

In this chapter we discussed some of the reasons why old people are abused or not cared for adequately in Indian families. Given this kind of problems, the problem of senior citizen abuse becomes widespread and also gets very little attention from the wider society. Hence, it becomes more important to raise awareness of such kinds of problems and the available remedies.

Chapter 5: Where to go for help

In this chapter, we go through some of the avenues and organizations where senior citizens, or those concerned for their welfare, can go for help and protection in case of abuse.

5.1 Local police station

The most natural place for senior citizens to go to in case of abuse is their local police station. It is the duty of the police to help vulnerable people in society such as senior citizens. The police can be reached by calling the special emergency telephone number 100 or 112 or by visiting the police station to register a police complaint, after which they may file an FIR.

However, this is the very place many senior citizens may be most reluctant to approach, either for fear of the police, unfamiliarity with the process of reporting crimes or fear of repercussions from the abusers who may be their own family members on whom they are dependent.

Sometimes in India, especially in smaller cities, the police may be corrupt or ask for bribes, or be reluctant to lodge an FIR to avoid extra work for themselves. Also, some senior citizens might equate going to the police with bringing shame on their family and so would be extra reluctant to report the abuse. Others might feel that their family members might be jailed by the police if they report the abuse incident, even though in practice this is very unlikely to happen. Some senior citizens may have lack of trust in the police, or be skeptical of the effectiveness of the police in delivering justice. For all these reasons, they do not approach the police and do not report the abuse incidents.

5.2 Senior citizen cells and helplines

In some big cities, there may exist some special helplines to report incidents of abuse. Sometimes, the local police themselves may set up such helplines. Senior citizens can call these helpline numbers in case of abuse, and they connect to a specialized police cell. All such helpline calls are usually logged, so chances of getting justice using these helplines is better. However, such senior citizen cells and helplines are not available in all cities, only in the big metro cities. The phone number 1090 is applicable for most senior citizen helplines, so it is worth trying this number.

Example Senior Citizen helpline numbers are as follows:

- 1091/1291 of Delhi Police Senior Citizen Helpline
- 1090 Elders helpline of Bangalore police.

5.3 Senior citizens tribunals

The Senior citizen tribunal is constituted for appeals related to Senior Citizens Act 2007. Such tribunals are available in many big cities in India and are usually under the district magistrate (DM) or the additional district magistrate (ADM) or Sub-Divisional Magistrate (SDM). The senior citizens should approach the DMs or ADMs with a written complaint about their abuse, in order to get the relief.

The Senior Citizens Protection Act, also called the Maintenance and Welfare of Parents and Senior Citizens Act, 2007, can be invoked by senior citizens to ask the courts or police for maintenance from their children and legal heirs in case they are destitute or homeless, or face threats to their life and well-being. However, the process of seeking redressal under this act can sometimes be complicated. The ADM/SDM might call a hearing where the senior citizens and the abusers have to face each other, which can be traumatic for some senior citizens.

Some links to senior citizen tribunals are as follows:

- Delhi Senior Citizens Tribunal: https://socialwelfare.delhigovt.nic.in/content/district-maintenance-tribunal-officers
- Bangalore Senior Citizens Tribunal: https://www.kaanoon.com/127612/details-of-senior-citizen-s-tribunal-in-bangalore

5.4 National Human Rights Commission (NHRC)

In cases where some government officials, such as police or others, are involved in the abuse, or the senior citizens are not being provided the services by government offices, they may file an online or offline complaint at the National Human Rights Commission or NHRC. The complaint to NHRC can be filed either online or in person, by visiting their office or by writing a letter and sending by registered post. There are also similar state human rights commissions in different states of India.

However, the NHRC website and platform for complaints is based online and is the preferred medium for complaints, so it might be difficult for senior citizens to use it if they are not adequately familiar with technology.

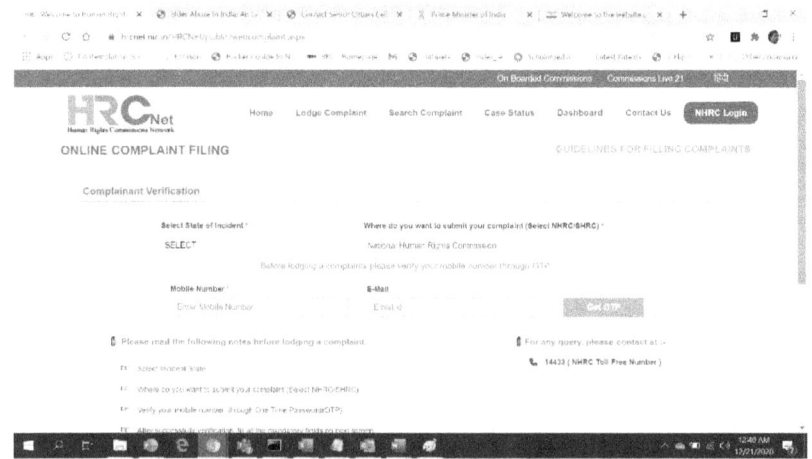

Figure: Interface for filing online complaints at the NHRC website

The NHRC website for how to file an online complaint and the complaints portal is as follows: https://nhrc.nic.in/complaints/complaints/how-to-file-a-complaints and https://www.hrcnet.nic.in/HRCNet/public/webcomplaint.aspx

5.5 National Commission for Women

NCW or National Commission for Women Cell is primarily meant for protecting women facing domestic violence and other kinds of abuse. It can, therefore, also help senior citizen women. The NCW website has a space for logging online complaints of abuse by women. The complaints first go through a verification process before they are accepted and given a registration number.

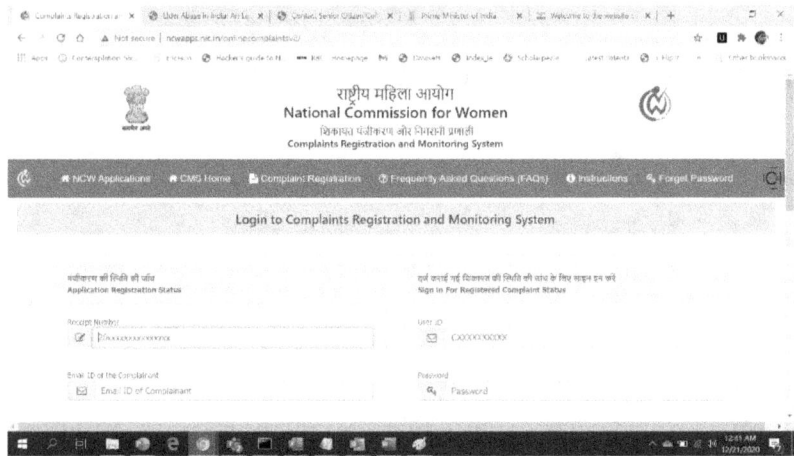

Figure: Interface for filing online complaints at the NCW website

The NCW website for logging online complaints is at the following link: http://ncwapps.nic.in/onlinecomplaintsv2/

Figure: NGOs working for senior citizens in India

5.6 Government Schemes for Senior Citizens

Several central government schemes provide financial, medical, and material support to senior citizens in India. While awareness of these schemes is low among many seniors, they can provide significant relief especially for those who cannot afford private healthcare or assistive devices.

Ayushman Bharat PM-JAY (Health Insurance)

As of 2024, the Ayushman Bharat Pradhan Mantri Jan Arogya Yojana has been expanded to cover all senior citizens aged 70 years and above with free health insurance of up to ₹5 lakh per year, irrespective of income. A separate Ayushman Vaya Vandana card is issued for this purpose. Eligible senior citizens can apply at any Common Service Centre (CSC), through the AB-PMJAY portal, or by calling the helpline 14555. This scheme directly addresses the unaffordability of private hospital treatment discussed in Chapter 2.

Rashtriya Vayoshri Yojana (Free Assistive Devices)

The Rashtriya Vayoshri Yojana (RVY) is a central government scheme that provides free assistive devices to senior citizens belonging to Below Poverty Line (BPL) families. Devices provided include walking sticks, elbow crutches, walkers, tripods, hearing aids, wheelchairs, artificial dentures, and spectacles. The scheme is implemented by the Artificial Limbs Manufacturing Corporation of India (ALIMCO) in collaboration with state governments. Senior citizens who are unable to afford these aids — which are essential for maintaining independence and dignity in daily life — can enquire about camps held in their district through their local District Social Welfare Office or through the Ministry of Social Justice helpline.

National Helpline for Senior Citizens — Elderline 14567

The Elderline 14567, operated by the Ministry of Social Justice and Empowerment, is a free national helpline available from 8 AM to 8 PM daily across all states and union territories. Beyond crisis support, it also helps senior citizens enrol in government schemes, access pension and financial entitlements, find old age homes, and receive referrals for legal and medical help. Senior citizens who are unsure which government scheme they may be eligible for are encouraged to call 14567 as a first step.

5.7 Senior citizen Non-Governmental Organizations or NGOs

There are a few NGOs focused on helping senior citizens, both nationally and in different cities. Examples of such organizations include HelpAge India, Dignity Foundation, Agewell Foundation, and Harmony. We will study them in detail in a following chapter. Such NGOs can be a useful support group for senior citizens, as they might give a sympathetic hearing to them and also connect them with the local police, old age homes and other services.

The websites of some of these NGOs are as follows:

- Helpage India: https://www.helpageindia.org/
- Dignity Foundation. https://dignityfoundation.com/
- Agewell Foundation https://www.agewellfoundation.org/

- Harmony https://www.harmonyindia.org/

5.8 Local MPs, MLAs and other politicians

In some cases, though not all cases, the local politicians of different political parties, or members of parliament (MPs) and members of legislative assembly (MLAs) living in the area might be able to help in case of abuse. The senior citizens or their well-wishers should find out the contacts or offices of the local politicians and visit them or write letters to explain their situation and ask for help or protection.

- The website https://www.contactminister.com/ has the contact details of various members of parliament in India
- The website https://www.india.gov.in/my-government/whos-who/mlasmlcs gives a list of all the MLAs in different states of India.

5.9 Local or national newspapers

Another possible avenue for senior citizens to highlight their issues is the print and digital media, such as local newspapers in English, Hindi or regional languages. Many of these newspapers have a space for readers to send letters to the editor, which can be physical letters or by email. Generally, the email addresses for writing to the editor are mentioned in the newspapers in the same place where the letters are published. The writer should mention his or her full name, mailing address and subject of the letter.

For some example newspapers, the contacts are as follows:

- The Hindu newspaper, the email address for letters to the editor is letters@thehindu.co.in
- The email for Hindustan Times is letters@hindustantimes.com and Hindustan (Hindi newspaper) is mailbox@livehindustan.com

However, this avenue of writing to Indian newspapers is more likely to succeed if the letters are related to some recently published article or highlight the social problem of senior citizens abuse in more general terms, along with recommendations of what can be done as a society to stop such incidents. Letters mentioning individual cases of abuses may not get accepted to be published.

5.10 Old age homes

In case of severe issues such as homelessness due to being abandoned by their children, senior citizens may try to contact old age homes. These have dedicated living spaces and employees to take care of the elderly people. However, the kind of facilities provided may vary. Many of them may also need regular monthly payments for senor citizens to stay there.

Source:

- Rhythm Sachdeva, Give India, October 2019. 10 old age homes in India for abandoned senior citizens https://blog.giveindia.org/elderly/10-old-age-homes-in-india-for-abandoned-senior-citizens/
- Senior Indian. List of old age homes in India (State wise).

- https://www.seniorindian.com/old_age_homes_list.htm
- Dada Dadi Organization. Directory of old age homes in India. http://dadadadi.org/old-age-homes-in-India.html

5.11 Free or Low-cost legal advice websites

There are a number of websites available for getting free or low-cost legal advice from lawyers in India. Such websites can be used by senior citizens in case of need. However, they do require familiarity with technology to log their question online.

The procedure to log a legal query is as follows: one has to visit the website, create a free account by filling some basic details. After that, one can log one's query, which will be answered by the lawyers within a few hours. Some of the advocates may send private messages or directly call the person logging the complaint, rather than reply on the public forum. Also, they may ask for a fee for their advice, or pressurize the person to hire them as a lawyer.

Examples of free legal advice websites include the following:

- Lawrato: https://lawrato.com/free-legal-advice
- Indian Kanoon https://www.kaanoon.com/
- Vkeel https://www.vkeel.com/
- Vidhikarya https://www.vidhikarya.com/

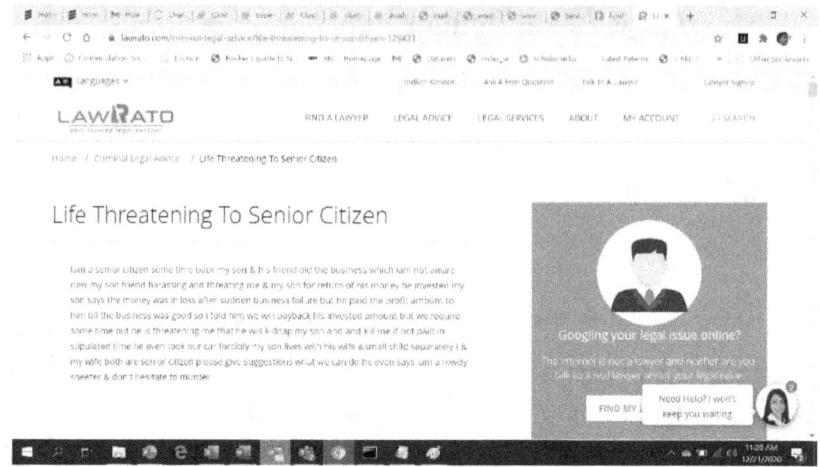

Figure: Screenshot for a complaint related to senior citizen abuse logged on the lawrato website

Of these, Lawrato seems to have many lawyers relying to each query promptly and in the public. Indian Kanoon is a very good resource for accessing past court judgements on various topics.

5.12 Prime Minister's Office and President's Secretariat

The senior citizens can also directly approach the prime minister's office with their complaints and grievances. There is a dedicated website to write to the Hon. Prime Minister. They may also accept physical letters of complaints or grievances by Indian citizens. The complaints received at the PMO are then forwarded to respective departments to investigate further and resolve the issues.

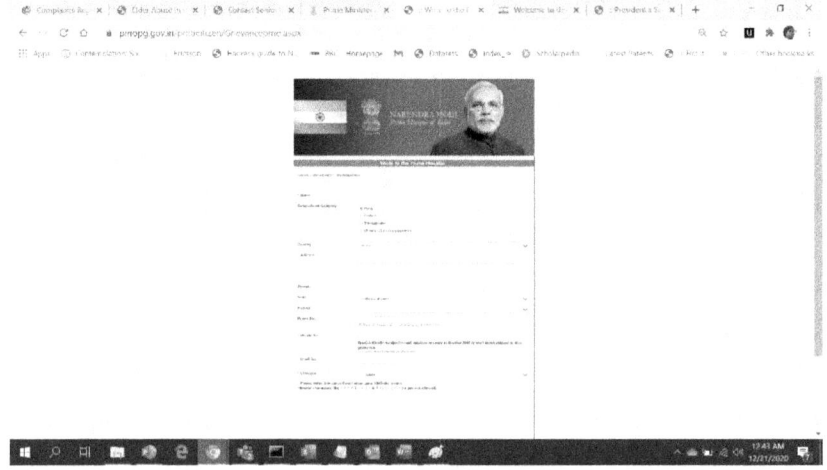

Figure: Interface for filing an online grievance at the PMO website

The website to log grievances at the PMO (prime minister office) is as follows: https://pmopg.gov.in/pmocitizen/Grievancepmo.aspx

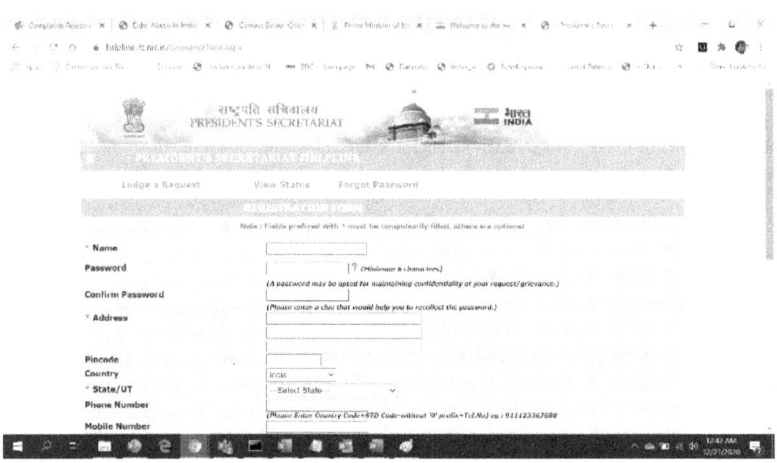

Figure: Interface for filing an online request or grievance at the President's secretariat

Similarly, a grievance can be raised with the secretariat of the President of India. They also have an online portal. They may also be able to accept physical letters. The website is as follows: https://helpline.rb.nic.in/GrievanceNew.aspx

5.13 Senior Citizen Associations

Many cities in India have senior citizen associations, where the senior citizens in local communities come together, socialize and discuss their problems. They can be found in both big and small cities. Such organizations can also be a valuable source of support when one is faced with abuse. They often work with NGOs and other organizations to coordinate support to needy senior citizens. It is a good idea for senior citizens to join such organizations.

Some of the associations are as follows:

- All India senior citizens confederation AISCCON: https://www.aisccon.org/
- Senior citizens council of Delhi http://seniorcitizensdelhi.org/
- Senior citizens support forum http://scsforum.org
- Tamil Nadu senior citizens association http://www.tanseca.com/
- Association of senior living India http://www.asli.org.in/

5.14 Mental Health Support and Counselling

Abuse takes a severe psychological toll on senior citizens. Studies indicate that approximately 1 in 3 elderly Indians experiences symptoms of depression, which is strongly associated with neglect, social isolation, and lack of emotional support from children. Many senior citizens who are being abused are not ready to file a formal police complaint or approach a tribunal — but they urgently need someone to talk to. Counselling services offer a confidential, non-threatening first step.

The Elderline helpline 14567 provides psychosocial counselling in addition to legal and scheme guidance. The NGO helplines listed in Chapter 8 — including HelpAge India (1800-180-1253) and Dignity Foundation (city-specific numbers) — also offer emotional support to senior citizens. For senior citizens comfortable with technology, the iCall service by TISS (Tata Institute of Social Sciences) offers tele-counselling at low or no cost: website icallhelpline.org, phone 9152987821. Vandrevala Foundation runs a 24-hour mental health helpline at 1860-2662-345, which is available in multiple languages including Hindi.

Family members and caregivers should be attentive to the warning signs of depression in elderly relatives: persistent sadness or withdrawal, loss of appetite, reluctance to engage in activities they previously enjoyed, increased anxiety or fearfulness, and expressions of hopelessness. These symptoms are not simply a natural part of ageing — they are treatable, and appropriate support can significantly improve quality of life. Encouraging an elderly relative to speak to a counsellor, even anonymously through a helpline, can be a valuable first step.

5.15 Conclusion

In this chapter, we have looked at some organizations and places where the senior citizens can raise complaints about abuse and seek relief or help. It is good for senior citizens to keep a printed list of such places as well as a list of helpline numbers, such as the senior citizens helplines.

Chapter 6: Senior Citizens Protection Act

Senior Citizens Protection Act is also called the Maintenance and Welfare of Parents and Senior Citizens Act, 2007.

In this chapter, we discuss this senior citizens protection act and ways to seek redressal by senior citizens who are being abused or neglected by their own children and in a state of poverty. We also discuss some of the state-wise rules for implementation of the act in different states in India.

Note: 2019 Amendment to the Act

The Maintenance and Welfare of Parents and Senior Citizens (Amendment) Act, 2019 was passed by Parliament, expanding the definition of "children" to include son-in-law and daughter-in-law, widening the scope of "maintenance," and increasing the maximum monthly maintenance amount from Rs 10,000 to Rs 20,000. The amendment also strengthens provisions for protection of life and property of senior citizens and makes abandonment of a senior citizen a punishable offence with increased penalties. Readers should check whether the 2019 Amendment has been notified and enforced in their particular state, as implementation may vary.

Figure: Cover page of the Senior Citizens Act 2007

6.1 What is covered in the act

The Senior Citizens Protection Act is primarily intended to protect senior citizen parents from abandonment by their family members and obliges the sons and legal heirs of senior citizens to take care of them, by actions such as providing a monthly maintenance allowance. It is enforced by senior citizen tribunals under the DMs or SDMs, who can pass maintenance orders.

The act also talks about:

- establishment of old age homes in every district

- provision of medical care by reserving beds for senior citizens in government hospitals
- provisions by respective state governments to be enacted for the protection of life and property of senior citizens.

The first two clauses of the act are as follows:

A senior citizen including parent who is unable to maintain himself from his own earning or property owned by him, shall be entitled to make an application under section 5 in case of –

• parent or grand-parent, against one or more of his children not being a minor

• a childless senior citizen, against such of his relative referred to in clause (g) of section 2

The obligation of the children or relative, as the case may be, to maintain a senior citizen extends to the needs of such citizen so that senior citizen may lead a normal life.

An application for maintenance under section 4, may be made -

- by a senior citizen or a parent, as the case may be; or
- if he is incapable, by any other person or organisation authorised by him; or
- the Tribunal may take cognizance suo motu

6.2 How to approach for help

This act can be invoked by senior citizens by approaching the senior citizen tribunals in their respective state, asking for maintenance from their children or relatives in case of inadequate income to support themselves, loss of residence or other needs.

The maintenance and other protections ordered under this act are to be enforced by senior citizens maintenance tribunals in various cities and in every state, which are usually under the ADM, SDM or district magistrates.

The typical procedure to approach them includes the following steps:

- The senior citizens file a written complaint. They may also approach the office and explain their situation with a verbal complaint as well.
- The complaint is submitted at the tribunal or the office of the DM/SDM/ADM of that area or district.
- The authorities process the complaint and may call a hearing, at which the alleged abusers are also invited.
- During the hearing, both sides must approach without any lawyers. The senior citizens can then explain the situation, especially the abuse in detail, in front of the DM or SDM. They are given a patient hearing. The alleged abusers also get a chance to respond. Unfortunately, in some cases this may turn into a shouting match.
- After the hearing, the DM or SDM passes a judgment, which could include an order for the abusers to pay a monthly sum of maintenance to the senior citizen. This may also include other orders, such as a warning

to the abusers to not abuse the senior citizens any more.

6.3 Problems with accessing relief under the Senior Citizens act

Even though the senior citizen parents can claim maintenance under the act, the procedure process of seeking redressal under this act can sometimes be time consuming, bureaucratic and expensive. The senior citizens might have to approach the tribunals and sometimes the courts for the purpose of claiming maintenance, which can be daunting. Also, the maintenance amount granted may sometimes be inadequate for supporting the medical and other costs of the senior citizens. Moreover, just granting a certain sum of money and not other kinds of necessary support may not be enough for their needs.

Hence, there is a need to have simpler, inexpensive and speedy provisions to claim maintenance for senior citizen parents.

6.4 Links to more information about the Senior Citizens Protection Act

The following are some links to more information about the act:

- Wikipedia page about the Act https://en.wikipedia.org/wiki/Maintenance_and_Welfare_of_Parents_and_Senior_Citizens_Act,_2007
- Senior Citizens Protection Act soft copy, downloadable as PDF:

http://wbja.nic.in/wbja_adm/files/The%20Maintenance%20and%20Welfare%20of%20Parents%20and%20Senior%20Citizens%20Act,%202007.pdf

6.5 Odisha Maintenance of Parents and Senior Citizens Rules, 2009

Figure: Cover page of the Orissa Maintenance of Parents and Senior Citizens Rules 2009

Orissa or Odisha has a separate set of rules about the procedure for parents to claim maintenance, as per the powers conferred on states in the senior citizens act 2007, which is applicable all over India. These rules are called the Orissa Maintenance of Parents and Senior Citizens Rules, 2009.

Online version: https://odishapolice.gov.in/sites/default/files/PDF/The%20Orissa%20Maintenance%20of%20Parents%20%26%20Senior%20Citizens%20Rules%2C2009..pdf

6.6 Karnataka Maintenance of Parents and Senior Citizens Rules, 2009

Karnataka too has specified rules in accordance with the Senior Citizens act 2007. These rules specify the detailed procedures under which to claim maintenance by senior citizen parents and what to do if the respondence do not appear, appeals process, establishment of old age homes and so on.

The Karnataka rules are available online here: https://www.lawyerservices.in/Karnataka-Maintenance-and-Welfare-of-Parents-and-Senior-Citizens-Rules-2009

6.7 Maharashtra Maintenance of Parents and Senior Citizens Rules, 2010

The Maharashtra state rules are available online here:

Online version: https://www.latestlaws.com/bare-acts/state-acts-rules/maharashtra-state-laws/maharashtra-maintenance-and-welfare-of-parents-and-senior-citizens-rules-2010/

6.8 Delhi Maintenance and Welfare of Parents and Senior Citizens (Amendment Rules), 2010

Online version: https://socialwelfare.delhigovt.nic.in/sites/default/files/All-PDF/Rules_0.pdf

6.9 The Assam State Maintenance and Welfare of Parents and Senior Citizens Rules, 2012

Online version: http://www.bareactslive.com/NER/ner218.htm

6.10 The Andhra Pradesh Maintenance and Welfare of Parents and Senior Citizens Rules, 2011

Online Version: http://wcdsc.tg.nic.in/documents/maintenance_senior_citizens_act.PDF

6.11 The Kerala Maintenance and Welfare of Parents and Senior Citizens Rules, 2009

Online version: http://www.bareactslive.com/KER/ker002.htm

Other states also have their own respective versions, although not all may be available online.

6.12 Conclusion

In this chapter, we have discussed the senior citizens maintenance act, some provisions of the act, how to apply for relief under the act and some versions of rules related to the maintenance and welfare of parents and senior citizens followed by different states in India.

Chapter 7: Senior citizen helplines

In this chapter, we discuss existing helplines for senior citizens in different cities, set up by the local police or by various charity organizations.

These helplines are ideally supposed to be available 24 hours, but some of them may be operated between 10 am-5 pm or working hours only. A senior citizen who calls these helplines might expect to hear a sympathetic and patient hearing of their problems of abuse, and possible action to help them seek redressal. As such, they are an important means of help for senior citizens who are in urgent trouble or being currently abused by their relatives or neighbors.

7.1 Police helplines against senior citizen abuse

In many but not all cities, 1090 serves as the main senior citizen helpline by the police. So even if it is not specifically listed it is worth trying to dial 1090 from any state or city in India.

- Gujarat Police Help line 1096
- Bengaluru police Senior Citizen Helpline 1090
- Chandigarh Police Senior Citizen Helpline 1090
- Delhi Police Senior Citizen Helpline 1291 and 1091
- Kolkata Police Senior Citizen Helpline 98300 88884
- Mumbai Police Senior Citizen Helpline 1090
- Pune Police Senior Citizen Helpline 1091

These helplines have been a success in providing timely help to senior citizens. In Bangalore, for example, the 1090 helpline run by the city police and Nightingale's Trust gets on average 40 calls daily.

7.2 Delhi police senior citizens cell

Delhi Police has a dedicated senior citizens cell, whom the senior citizens can approach in order to report abuse. This can be used in addition to the helpline number 1291 of the Delhi police.

Senior citizens can directly visit the office and lodge their complaints, or write to them with full details.

The contact details of the Delhi police senior citizens cell are as follows:

Delhi Police Senior Citizens Cell

Office : 1st Floor, Police Headquarters, M.S.O. Building, I.P.Estate, New Delhi.

Website : http://www.delhipolice.nic.in/seniorcitizen/index.html

e-mail : scscphq@bol.net.in

Delhi police also has an app for senior citizens, with an SOS button to contact in case of emergencies. It is meant to help senior citizens who are living alone. They can register their profile on the app or on the Delhi police senior citizen website.

Android store link to the app "Delhi Police Senior Citizen": https://play.google.com/store/apps/details?id=com.pcsolutions.samparkorsampadan

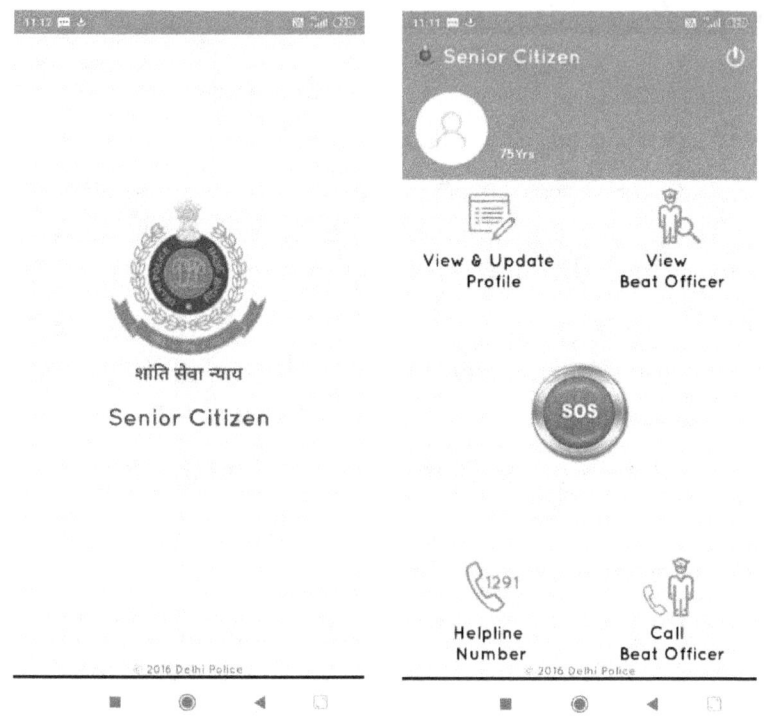

Figure: Screenshots from the Delhi police senior citizens app

7.3 Odisha Police senior citizens security cell

Odisha police has set up senior citizen security cells, along with the 1090 helpline. These cells are set up in all districts of Odisha. Along with other activities, they do verification of domestic servants of senior citizens in the police stations.

The website is https://odishapolice.gov.in/?q=node/6

7.4 List of helplines by Dada Dadi Organization and others

Dada Dadi organization has a comprehensive list of helplines in various cities, including both the police and voluntary organizations working for senior citizens. Some of these helplines can also provide legal advice when necessary, or put the senior citizen in contact with their lawyer who can help them to file cases in courts.

The link to the helplines is http://dadadadi.org/senior-citizen-helpline.html

The list includes not only the police helplines, but also the ones run by the senior citizen NGOs such as Dignity Foundation, HelpAge India and so on.

Dignity foundation helplines are available in six cities as follows:

- Mumbai Dignity Helpline +91 22 6138 1111
- Chennai Dignity Helpline +91 44 2621 0363
- Kolkata Dignity Helpline +91 92323 82936 / +91 91635 09818
- Bengaluru Dignity Helpline +91 96322 44568 / +91 97405 52261
- Pune Dignity Helpline +91 88304 49043
- Delhi Dignity Helpline +91 84483 17316

The HelpAge India helpline number is 1800-180-1253, which is a toll free number and applicable across India.

Some other helplines are as follows:

- Delhi Dada Dadi Help Foundation helpline: +(91)-9212717171 | 9212050505 | 26260777
- Madhya Pradesh Dada Dadi helpline: 99778 85999
- Hyderabad Senior Citizen Helpline 0901 047 0724 Prasanthi Karunamaya-Organisation
- Telangana government helpline for senior citizens 14567

Note that 14567 is registered as a nationwide helpline for senior citizens. It is worth trying it from any city even if not in Telangana, to see if it is functional.

7.5 Conclusion

In this chapter, we have briefly discussed some of the available helplines for senior citizens in different Indian cities and pan India helplines run by different welfare organizations.

Chapter 8: Non-Governmental Organizations or NGOs working with Senior citizens

In this chapter, we discuss a few of the main NGOs that are working to help senior citizens in India. Many of these NGOs run their own helplines for senior citizens in different cities. A senior citizen can either call them, email them or walk into their offices and chat to the counsellors about their problems including abuse. They provide a sympathetic and patient hearing to the problems of senior citizens specifically, and so fulfil a vital social function.

Give the variety of problems faced by senior citizens, the NGOs can be a very valuable source of support. The helplines run by the NGOs complement the police run helplines. The NGOs typically provide support and counselling for all aspects of the senior citizens' lives, not just in cases of abuse. Their support extends to the mental and physical health issues, financial issues, legal issues, destitution, homelessness, property disputes and so on.

8.1 HelpAge India

HelpAge India is one of the largest NGOs working for the welfare of senior citizens. They were established in 1978, run a variety of programs for senior citizens. Their programs include cancer care, cataract surgeries, supporting destitute elders, running senior citizen helplines etc. They have contacts among police and lawyers who can assist the senior citizens in legal cases. They have run numerous surveys and compiled reports of the extent of the problem of senior citizen abuse in India.

They have branches in different cities of India, with the main branch in New Delhi. They have collaborations with other international organizations working to help the elderly. They have won numerous awards for their activities, including Bharat Nirman Award, 2020 UN Population Award and Times Social Impact Award.

Head Office address: Address: 17, Tara Crescent Road, Qutab Institutional Area, New Delhi, 110016, Delhi, India Phone: +91 11 4168 8955

Figure: Homepage of the HelpAge India website

Links to websites for more information
- https://www.helpageindia.org/
- https://en.wikipedia.org/wiki/HelpAge_India

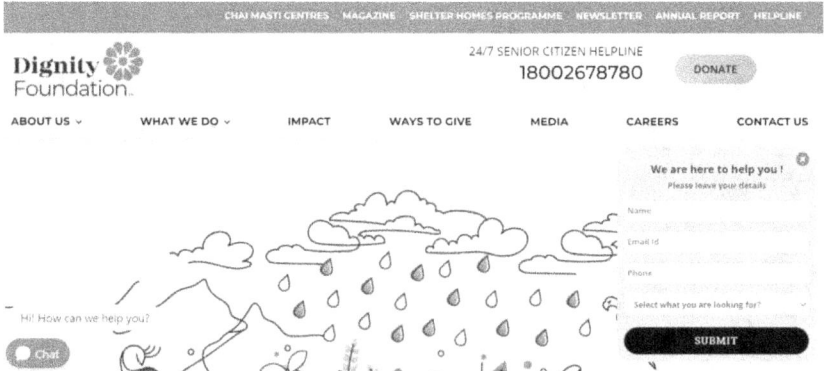

Figure: Screenshot of the Dignity Foundation homepage

8.2 Dignity Foundation

Dignity foundation was established in 1995 in Mumbai, originally starting as a magazine called Dignity Dialogue. and now have branches in many cities. They also run city specific helplines for senior citizens in six cities of India and growing. They run a wide variety of programs benefitting senior citizens.

Head office address: Dignity Foundation, B-206, 2nd Floor, Byculla Service Industries Premises Sussex Road, Byculla (E) Mumbai - 400 027

Telephone : 6138 1100

Email : responsedignity@dignityfoundation.com

Websites : www.dignityfoundation.com / www.dignitylifestyle.org

Figure: Screenshot of the homepage of the Agewell foundation

8.3 Agewell Foundation

Agewell Foundation has association NGO status with United Nations (UN) DPI. It was set up in 1999. They run various activities like healthcare campaigns and training programs. They conduct research into the problems faced by senior citizens, as well as advocate for welfare measures for senior citizens. They interact with over 25000 senior citizens on a daily basis.

Office address: M-8A, Lajpat Nagar-II, New Delhi-110024, India

Phone : +91-29836486, +91-29840484, +91-29830005

Fax : 011-29840484

E-mail : agewellfoundation@gmail.com

Website : www.agewellfoundation.org

8.4 Dada Dadi

Dada Dadi is an organization for senior citizens that is based in Chandigarh. It runs various helplines and advocacy on behalf of senior citizens. It has a very comprehensive website with a good listing of rights and support services available for senior citizens in India.

Website: https://www.dadadadi.org/

8.5 Harmony

This organization was initially launched in 2004 as a magazine called Harmony magazine, which is still running. It is based in Mumbai.

Website: https://www.harmonyindia.org/

8.6 List of other organizations

A list of a few other NGOs is as below. However, there are many other NGOs too for senior citizens, as well as many NGO who might not be specifically for senior citizens, also work for their welfare.

- Devamitra foundation https://www.devamitra.org/old-age-ngo-india/

- Sneh foundation https://www.facebook.com/Sneh-Foundation-136083433482227/

8.7 Conclusion

In this chapter, we have briefly discussed the various non-governmental organizations to help senior citizens in different cities of India.

Chapter 9: Problems in Accessing Help and Strategies to Overcome the Problems

In this chapter, we discuss a few problems and obstacles that senior citizens commonly face when they try to report abuse to the authorities. We also cover a few legal strategies that senior citizens can use to protect themselves and overcome the problems.

As mentioned previously, there are a number of senior citizen helplines in India where senior citizens can turn to for help regarding abuse and other problems. 14567 is the nationwide helpline for senior citizens, 1291 (1090 in some other cities) is the senior citizen helpline, 112 is the emergency services including police, NGOs like HelpAge India, Dignity Foundation, AgeWell Foundation etc have their own helplines. In addition, senior citizens are free to access the courts for help as well as the additional district magistrates for help under Maintenance and Welfare of Parents and Senior Citizens Act, 2007.

However, in practice, there is still a wide gap between the availability of services and the senior citizens actually getting the help which they need. Our own personal experience has shown that often someone does answer the helplines but the police do not follow up with the actual help or confronting the abusers. In this article, we analyze some of the reasons for these gaps that prevent help from being given in a timely way.

One challenge in this can be due to the need of technology awareness to collect the evidence properly and file the complaints in the first place, which may hamper the process of getting help. They may be unaware of the helpline numbers or lose them, they may not be able to collect timely evidence such as documentation of medical needs or videos or photos of abuse or harassment, they may be suffering from memory loss and so on.

9.1 Problems with police

Many times, the police are reluctant to file FIRs or act on the abuse complaints, even when abuse is reported by senior citizens.

This may be due to several reasons such as the following:

- Corruption by the police
- Police wanting to avoid extra work
- Abuser being an influential person
- Police wanting to take bribes from the abused senior citizen before filing any case
- Police having taken bribes from the abusers
- Reported crime details from the senior citizens being vague
- Police believing it is difficult to collect evidence for the alleged crimes by the senior citizens
- Alleged crime not being in the police station jurisdiction
- Police not sensitized to take senior citizens seriously
- Police concluding non cognizable offence without a proper investigation

For example, in case of abuse of senior citizens related to ongoing property disputes, the police may close the case and not act citing that property disputes are beyond their jurisdiction.

Given that senior citizens are often reluctant to approach the police for several reasons, this perceived or real inaction by the police can have a compounding effect on the reporting and prevention of senior citizen abuse. Hence, it should be combated.

9.1.1 Example where police did not take senior citizen abuse complaints seriously

The following extract from a newspaper shows how police inaction may work in case of senior citizen abuse, and a possible remedy to approach the courts to force the police to act.

The Hindu, Dec 21, 2020: Delhi HC orders police protection for senior citizen couple. Duo claims assault by daughter, her husband

The Delhi High Court has ordered the city police to ensure sufficient protection for a senior citizen couple who claimed that they were being "tormented and physically beaten" by their daughter and son-in-law living with them.

Justice Vibhu Bakhru said the couple can also approach their area District Magistrate under Rule 22 of Delhi Maintenance and Welfare of Parents and Senior Citizens Rules (DMWPSCR) for their protection. Rule 22 of DMWPSCR lays down guidelines for protection of life and

property of senior citizens. It says that complaints of senior citizens shall be promptly attended to by the local police.

'Police inaction': The High Court's order came while hearing the plea of a 67-year-old man and his wife who said the police have not taken any effective steps to protect them despite several complaints. The man, who claimed to be suffering from paralysis and old-age ailments, said that on October 12 he was beaten up by his daughter. He had called the police and some officers had visited the premises. However, they did not take any action and asked the couple to submit a written complaint. He alleged that their statements were also not recorded. Thereafter, on December 13, his daughter and son-in-law once again assaulted them, claimed the complainant. The Delhi government's Additional Standing Counsel submitted that the complaints received from the old couple do not reflect any cognisable offence and are largely regarding unpleasantness and petty squabbles between the family members. The counsel, however, assured the court that the concerned beat staff will visit the complainants' residence on a daily basis and ensure that they are not brought to any harm.

9.1.2 Strategies with the police

In case the police do not register complaints properly without investigation or else close the complaints too soon, the following strategies can be used by senior citizens and their well-wishers:

- Approach senior citizen cells, if available in their city

- File Right to Information Requests (RTIs) to the inspectors or higher up police officers, to get the police to act on their specific complaints of abuse
- Always file written complaints to the police rather than verbal. One can also file e-complaints in the police website, if the facility is available.
- One can use twitter or other social media to highlight their complaint, tagging the police cell in their city
- If possible, collect evidence of abuse, such as video or audio clips, hospital reports of injuries from a government hospital
- Send the complaints to the police and other agencies by registered post or speed post, keeping a record of their sending
- Approach the courts to force the police to register FIRs
- Approach the senior citizens NGOs, such as HelpAge India or Dignity Foundation, for help
- Approach the National Commission for Women (NCW) in case of non-action by the police and if the abused is a woman
- Approach the National Human Rights Commission India (NHRC) with evidence of past correspondence and non-action by the police

9.2 Problems with senior citizen helplines

Although it is good that helplines are available for abused senior citizens in different cities of India. Many of these helplines are run by the Senior Citizen NGOs. However, even these helplines suffer from some practical problems. Some of the problems are as follows:

- Often, the senior citizens might not be able to articulate the problem of abuse accurately.
- Senior citizens may suffer from memory loss or dementia and not be able to recount the full details of the abuse accurately.
- Senior citizens may not be able to collect evidence about the abuse, given their lack of familiarity with technology.
- Since the senior citizens are often living with and dependent on the abuser, they may not tell the full story for fear of the abuse becoming worse.
- Senior citizens may be currently scared of threats made by the abusers, who may be their family members, even if they are not living with them.
- Sometimes the police might be reluctant to lodge FIRs or take action, even after the abuse is reported.
- In some cities, especially the smaller cities, the police might be corrupt and take bribes from the abusers and suppress the investigation.
- In some cases, the abusers may be influential people who may be able to put pressure on the police.
- Helplines run by the NGOs, since they do not have official powers and are not directly linked to the police, might not be able to do much in case of abuses or threats, other than reporting the abuse to the local police.

Because of all these reasons, the effectiveness of the available help for senior citizens may be reduced. This should be kept in mind by policy makers, police and the people running the helplines. They should be better sensitized and more responsive to the problems faced by senior citizens. More importantly, while the first level response to the helplines may be there, the follow up support might be lacking. There should be a proper plan to fix this gap and make the helplines more effective.

It is important for the persons running the helplines to be extra sensitive to the senior citizens issues, give them a patient hearing and the best advice to move forward to prevent the abuse.

9.2.1 Strategies to fix issues with the senior citizen helplines

The following can be some strategies to follow if a call to the helpline number, especially if the helpline is run by the police, is not useful:

- Follow up the helpline call with a written complaint
- Send the written complaint by registered post/ speed post and email.
- Contact the police senior citizen cell, if it exists
- Follow the other strategies as mentioned in the previous section in case of problems with the police

9.3 Problems with lawyers and judiciary

Sometimes the abused senior citizen may have no option but to take the help of the judiciary to enforce their rights and prevent abuse. This can be necessary in case of property disputes, such as when a son or neighbor is trying to take hold of the property by force, or in case of wills. This can also be needed when the police do not act on a written complaint by the senior citizen. In such cases, the senior citizen may have to hire a lawyer to send a legal notice or file a case on the abuser.

However, hiring a lawyer or filing a case may lead to several problems of its own, including the following:

- Senior citizens may not know the legal process and depend completely on the lawyer
- Lawyer may overcharge the senior citizens
- The lawyer may accept bribes from the abusive party and misrepresent the case
- Lawyer may be incompetent or inexperienced
- Lawyer may treat the senior citizen as an easy income source and not take the case seriously
- Lawyer may advise the senior citizen to file multiple unnecessary cases, just because they get extra money per filing
- The property dispute cases may continue for months or years
- While the case is going on in the courts, there is no respite for the senior citizen and the abuses may continue

9.3.1 Strategies with the lawyers

Some of the strategies for senior citizens to prevent the problems with the lawyers are as follows:

- Consult several lawyers before deciding to hire one
- Put the case or abuse details on an online site like lawrato.com to get the opinions of various lawyers

- Hire a lawyer who has some experience, if possible check their credentials or qualifications online
- Hire lawyers who are familiar with technology and keeps themselves abreast of the latest developments, ideally they should not be too old
- Hire lawyers who do the case work themselves rather than relying on too many assistants
- Negotiate the rate with the lawyer in advance and insist on paying in installments, dependent on the progression of the case
- In case the lawyer pressurizes the senior citizens to settle or to file extra cases, the senior citizens should do their own research before deciding, b consulting multiple people
- Make yourself familiar with the court process by visiting courts, talking to people, reading past judgments and so on.

9.4 Use of RTI Act

The Right to Information Act (RTI), 2015 is an Act of the Parliament of India "to provide for setting out the practical regime of right to information for citizens." The RTI Act allows citizens of India, including senior citizens, to request information from any public authority about its work and actions. This act is a very useful tool that can be used by senior citizens in case of inaction by police or other institutions in response to reports of abuse or other problems. It must be noted that the RTI act is mainly applicable for public data, such as data in the public domain or data related to actions by government officials or police.

It cannot be used generally for data related to private companies.

The act comprises filing an RTI application (online or on paper) with the correct authority (state or central government) on whom the information request is to be made. There is a time limit within which the authority has to respond to the information request under RTI, and the person can file an appeal if they are not satisfied with the response.

The RTI process includes the following:

- The citizen files an RTI request either online or by postal mail to the central or state government department concerned, paying the required fees (nominal charges of Rs 10) and submitting the necessary documents.
- The query or request for information goes to the Commissioner or public information officer of the state or center depending on whom the RTI has been requested, who then forwards the query to the concerned department.
- The department has to submit a reply to the citizen's query within 30 days.
- There is also appeals process as part of the RTI. The citizen can file an appeal in the prescribed form if the reply received is not satisfactory.

To file an RTI request, one needs to go to the RTI portal for the central government or the state government. The central government RTI portal is https://www.rtionline.gov.in/ Nowadays, many third party tools and websites are also available that will fill an RTI request on payment of a small fee and filling all the details online.

For example, in case of inaction by the police to a written complaint of abuse, a senior citizen can file an RTI to the inspector or concerned police official, or their seniors, asking what action has been taken to their specific complaints. This puts pressure on the police or other authorities to act.

A sample RTI application is as follows:

To

The Central/Public Information Officer, RTI Office

(Address of public authority/Office)

Date:

Subject: Request to furnish information under Right to Information Act, 2005

Dear Sir/ Madam,

You are requested to furnish the following information/documents.

1.

2.

If the information is not available in your office, kindly forward to the concerned public authority as per section 6(3) of the RTI Act,2005.

I am a citizen of India and address is given below. Requisite RTI application fee for Rs.10/- paid via Indian Postal Order/ Bank Draft/ Cheque No.............. dated...................... is enclosed.

Yours sincerely,

(Name & Signature)

Address:

Some links to get more information on RTI and the process, are as follows:

• Wikipedia. Right to Information Act 2005 https://en.wikipedia.org/wiki/Right_to_Information_Act,_2005

• Information about RTI from experts https://onlinerti.com/about-rti

• Online RTI website https://www.rtionline.gov.in/

9.5. Conclusion

In this chapter we have discussed problems encountered by senior citizen when using the senior citizens helplines, police and lawyers, and also discussed some strategies to deal with these problems.

Chapter 10: Some practical tips

In this chapter, we discuss a few general tips on how to help or enable senior citizens to report abuse and protect themselves from abuse.

10.1 Awareness of rights of senior citizens

One of the things people can do to help their senior citizen relatives from threats and abuses is to make them aware of their rights and options for help, including police helpline numbers in various cities such as 1090. Same goes for awareness of the laws that protect them, such as the senior citizens protection act.

10.2 Training to use technology

Another way to help the senior citizens is to make them familiar with technology. This can include the following:

- Teaching them how to access the internet

- Teaching them to browse basic websites to find information

- Making sure they have internet on their smartphones and know how to use it etc.

10.3 Making senior citizens aware of helplines and other support

Another way to help senior citizens is to make them aware of the helplines, as well as give them a list of helpline numbers to call, such as numbers of NGOs, whenever an issue such as abuse occurs.

10.4 Changing ingrained mindsets among senior citizens

Changing ingrained mindsets of senior citizens, such as decreasing their ingrained fear of police and courts by gently explaining the procedures to approach them, can also go a long way for them to asset their rights and curb abuse by others. Same goes for awareness of things such as writing and registering a will for their property.

10.5 Avoiding domestic abuse

For married children of senior citizens, one of the ways of protecting their parents from abuse by their wives or other relatives can be simply to move out to a different house close by, yet ensuring that their parents have enough support when it comes to basic needs such as medical and psychological needs.

10.6 Education to change mindsets of young people

Young people can also be educated about the problems faced by older people. Such education can go a long way in solving inter generation conflicts and reducing the possibility of abuse of senior citizens.

10.7 Warning Signs: Are You Being Abused?

Many senior citizens do not recognise that what they are experiencing constitutes abuse, particularly when it involves family members. The following checklist may help identify a situation of abuse. You may be facing abuse if one or more of the following are true:

You are frequently afraid to speak freely at home, or feel that you must hide your feelings or opinions to avoid retaliation. Your money, bank accounts, or property are being accessed, controlled, or managed by someone else without your knowledge or consent. You are being denied basic necessities such as food, water, medicines, or clothing, whether deliberately or through neglect. You are being pressured to sign documents such as property transfers, gift deeds, bank forms, or a will that you do not understand or do not wish to sign. You have been threatened with abandonment, being sent to an old age home, or other consequences if you do not comply with someone's demands. You are not allowed to speak to friends, relatives, or neighbours without a family member being present. Your phone or internet access is being restricted or monitored. You are being humiliated, insulted, or verbally abused regularly. You have suffered physical injury caused by a family member or caregiver. You received a phone or video call from someone claiming to be a police officer or government official, who asked you to stay on the call and pay money.

If several of these apply to you, you are likely experiencing abuse and you should reach out for help. You can call the nationwide senior citizen helpline 14567, HelpAge India's toll-free helpline 1800-180-1253, or your local police helpline 1090. You do not need to file a formal complaint immediately — simply speaking to a counsellor at one of these helplines is a safe first step.

10.8 Survival Action Ladder: Step-by-Step If You Are Being Abused

If you are currently experiencing abuse, the following step-by-step action ladder provides a clear path from immediate safety to longer-term legal protection. It consolidates guidance from Chapters 5, 6, 7, and 9 of this book.

Step 1 — Ensure Immediate Safety. If you are in immediate physical danger, call the emergency number 112 or police helpline 100. If you need to leave the house, try to go to a trusted neighbour, a nearby relative, or a community space.

Step 2 — Call a Helpline. Call 14567 (national senior citizen helpline, 8 AM–8 PM), or HelpAge India at 1800-180-1253 (toll-free). These lines provide counselling, guidance, and referrals without requiring you to file a formal complaint immediately.

Step 3 — Tell a Trusted Person. Inform a trusted family member, friend, or neighbour about your situation. Having a witness or supporter is important for future steps. If the abuse is coming from within your own family, consider reaching out to a relative outside the household.

Step 4 — Document the Abuse. Keep a written record of incidents: dates, what happened, any injuries, and who was present. If possible, photograph injuries and keep copies of any documents you are being pressured to sign. Save any threatening messages. Ask your doctor to document injuries in a government hospital, as this creates an official record.

Step 5 — File a Written Complaint. Approach your local police station with a written complaint. Send copies by registered post and keep the postal receipt. If the police are unresponsive, approach the Senior Citizen Cell if one exists in your city. For financial abuse or property disputes, also file a complaint with the local Maintenance Tribunal (under the DM or SDM).

Step 6 — Approach the Maintenance Tribunal. Under the Maintenance and Welfare of Parents and Senior Citizens Act, 2007 (as amended in 2019), you can approach your district's Maintenance Tribunal to claim monthly maintenance, protection of your residence, or to reverse a property transfer made under duress. No lawyer is required for this process.

Step 7 — Escalate if Needed. If the police do not act, file an RTI asking what action has been taken on your complaint. Approach the National Human Rights Commission (NHRC) if government officials are unresponsive. Contact an NGO such as HelpAge India or Dignity Foundation for support and legal referrals. As a last resort, approach the High Court to direct the police to act.

10.9 Quick Reference: Key Helpline Numbers

It is recommended that senior citizens and their caregivers keep a printed copy of the following key numbers. These can be cut out or written on a card and kept in an accessible place.

112 — Police / Emergency (nationwide). 100 — Police (alternate). 1090 — Senior Citizen Helpline (most cities).

14567 — Senior Citizens Helpline (nationwide, try from any state). 1291 / 1091 — Delhi Police Senior Citizen Helpline. 1800-180-1253 — HelpAge India (toll-free, nationwide). Dignity Foundation (city-specific; see Chapter 7 for your city). Local ADM / SDM office — For maintenance claims under the Senior Citizens Act.

10.10 Conclusion

In this chapter, we have discussed some strategies that the youth and caretakers can use to help the senior citizens who are abused.

Chapter 11: Conclusion

In this book, we have looked at a few problems facing senior citizens in India, especially that of abuse and ill treatment by family members.

Reporting and combating abuse of senior citizens wherever we see it is only the first step.

11.1 Longer term solutions

The longer term solution for the problem of elder abuse is to raise awareness in society, show senior citizens in a positive light and highlight their problems, so that such incidents are prevented. This goes hand in hand with a better equipped health system to take care of the medical needs of senior citizens. Legal institutions have to be strengthened, along with simplified special court procedures, to make sure senior citizens face no difficulty in accessing legal help whenever they need it.

11.2 What the government can do

The government can play its role by increased support to senior citizens and sensitization of government employees, especially those who are service providers, to the problems faced by senior citizens. They should ensure the helplines are available in all cities big or small. There should be monitoring of the efficiency of the helplines to make sure they are effective in preventing abuse of different kinds. There should be increased government funding to senior citizens organizations, old age homes and NGOs, as well as in areas like healthcare and a comprehensive medical insurance for senior citizens. A major step was taken in 2024 when the Ayushman Bharat PM-JAY scheme was expanded to cover all senior citizens aged 70 and above with free health coverage of up to ₹5 lakh per year — this is a significant development that directly addresses the unaffordability of private healthcare for seniors. The government should build on this by making enrolment simpler and expanding coverage to senior citizens in private sector employment as well. Schemes for digitalization should keep in mind their potential impact on senior citizens who may not know technology. Equally, dedicated digital literacy programs for the elderly — including awareness about cyber fraud, OTP safety, and the 1930 helpline — should be made a national priority, given the rapid growth of scams targeting senior citizens.

11.3 Change in social attitudes

Many of the problems of elder abuse have its roots in other social problems, such as poverty, unemployment, lack of living spaces, inter generational gaps. To combat them we have to take responsibility as a society. The media, film industry, arts, and other industries have to play their part in highlighting the problems of modern lifestyles in which senior citizens often get caught up.

Abuse of senior citizens is a problem for all of us, and so we have to try and combat it together. Only by getting together and fighting the senior citizens abuse and taking steps to protect our senior citizens, can we make a better society in India.

Appendix A: THE MAINTENANCE AND WELFARE OF PARENTS AND SENIOR CITIZENS ACT, 2007

ACT NO. 56 OF 2007.

29 December, 2007.

An Act to provide for more effective provisions for the maintenance and welfare of parents and senior citizens guaranteed and recognised under the Constitution and for matters connected therewith or incidental thereto.

BE it enacted by Parliament in the Fifty-eighth Year of the Republic of India as follows:—

CHAPTER I: PRELIMINARY

1. **Short title, extent, application and commencement.**—(/)This Act may be called the Maintenance and Welfare of Parents and Senior Citizens Act, 2007.

(2) It extends to the whole of India except the State of Jammu and Kashmir and it applies also it citizens of India outside India.

(3) It shall come into force in a State on such date as the State Government may, by notification in the Official Gazette, appoint.

2. **Definitions.**—In this Act, unless the context otherwise requires,—

(a) "children" includes son, daughter, grandson and grand-daughter but does not include a minor;

(b) "maintenance" includes provisions for food, clothing, residence and medical attendance and treatment;

(c) "minor" means a person who, under the provisions of the Majority Act, 1875 (9 of 1875) is deemed not to have attained the age of majority;

(d) "parent" means father or mother whether biological, adoptive or step father or step mother, as the case may be, whether or not the father or the mother is a senior citizen;100

(e) "prescribed" means prescribed by rules made by the State Government under this Act;

(f) "property" means property of any kind, whether movable or immovable, ancestral or self acquired, tangible or intangible and includes rights or interests in such property;

(g) "relative" means any legal heir of the childless senior citizen who is not a minor and is in possession of or would inherit his property after his death;

(h) "senior citizen" means any person being a citizen of India, who has attained the age of sixty years or above;

(i) "State Government", relation to a Union territory, means the administrator thereof appointed under article 239 of the Constitution

(j) "Tribunal" means the Maintenance Tribunal constituted under section 7;

(k) "welfare" means provision for food, health care, recreation centres and other amenities necessary for the senior citizens.

3. **Act to have overriding effect**.—The provisions of this Act shall have effect notwithstanding anything inconsistent therewith contained in any enactment other than this Act, or in any instrument having effect by virtue of any enactment other than this Act.

CHAPTER II: MAINTENANCE OF PARENTS AND SENIOR CITIZENS

4. **Maintenance of parents and senior citizens** —A senior citizen including parent who is unable to maintain himself from his own earning or out of the property owned by him, shall be entitled to make an application under section 5 in case of—

(4) parent or grand-parent, against one or more of his children not being a minor;

(ii) a childless senior citizen, against such of his relative referred to in clause (g) of section 2.

(2) The obligation of the children or relative, as the case may be, to maintain a senior citizen extends to the needs of such citizen so that senior citizen may lead a normal life.

(3) The obligation of the children to maintain his or her parent extends to the needs of such parent either father or mother or both, as the case may be, so that such parent may lead a normal life.

(4) Any person being a relative of a senior citizen and having sufficient means shall maintain such senior citizen provided he is in possession of the property of such citizen or he would inherit the property of such senior citizen: Provided that where more than one relatives are entitled to inherit the property of a senior citizen, the maintenance shall be payable by such relative in the proportion in which they would inherit his property.

5. **Application for maintenance.**—An application for maintenance under section 4, may be made—

(a) by a senior citizen or a parent, as the case may be; or

(b) if he is incapable, by any other person or organisation authorised by him; or

(c) the Tribunal may take cognizance suo motu. Explanation—For the purposes of this section "organisation" means any voluntary association registered under the Societies Registration Act, 1860 (21 of 1860) or any other law for the time being in force.

(2) The Tribunal may, during the pendency of the proceeding regarding monthly allowance for the maintenance under this section, order such children or relative to make a monthly allowance for the interim maintenance of such senior citizen including parent and to pay the same to such senior citizen including parent as the Tribunal may from time to time direct.

(3) On receipt of an application for maintenance under subsection (J), after giving notice of the application to the children or relative and after giving the parties an opportunity of being heard, hold an inquiry for determining the amount of maintenance.

(4) An application filed under sub-section (2) for the monthly allowance for the maintenance and expenses for proceeding shall be disposed of within ninety days from the date of the service of notice of the application to such person: Provided that the Tribunal may extend the said period, once for a maximum period of thirty days in exceptional circumstances for reasons to be recorded in writing.

(5) An application for maintenance under sub-section (/) may be filled against one or more persons: Provided that such children or relative may

implead the other person liable to maintain parent in the application for maintenance.

(6) Where a maintenance order was made against more than one person, the death of one of them does not affect the liability of others to continue paying maintenance.

(7) Any such allowance for the maintenance and expenses for proceeding shall be payable from the date of the order, or, if so ordered, from the date of the application for maintenance or expenses of proceeding, as the case may be.

(8) If, children or relative so ordered fail, without sufficient cause to comply with the order, any such Tribunal may, for every breach of the order, issue a warrant for levying the amount due in the manner provided for levying fines, and may sentence such person for the whole, or any part of each month's allowance for the maintenance and expenses of proceeding, as the case be, remaining unpaid after the execution of the warrant, to imprisonment for a term which may extend to one month or until payment if sooner made whichever is earlier: Provided that no warrant shall be issued for the recovery of any amount due under this section unless application be made to the Tribunal to levy such amount within a period of three months from the date on which it became due.

6. **Jurisdiction and procedure**.— The proceedings under section 5 may be taken against any children or relative in any district—

(a) where he resides or last resided; or

(b) where children or relative resides.

(2) On receipt of the application under section 5, the Tribunal shall issues a process for procuring the presence of children or relative against whom the application is filed.

(3) For securing the attendance of children or relative the Tribunal shall have the power of a Judicial Magistrate of first class as provided under the Code of Criminal Procedure, 1973 (2 of 1974).

(4) All evidence to such proceedings shall be taken in the presence of the children or relative against whom an order for payment of maintenance is proposed to be made, and shall be recorded in the manner prescribed for summons cases: Provided that if the Tribunal is satisfied that the

children or relative against whom an order for payment of maintenance is proposed to be made is willfully avoiding service, or willfully neglecting to attend the Tribunal, the Tribunal may proceed to hear and determine the case ex parte.

(5) Where the children or relative is residing out of India, the summons shall be served by the Tribunal through such authority, as the Central Government may by notification in the official Gazette, specify in this behalf.

(6) The Tribunal before hearing an application under section 5 may, refer the same to a Conciliation Officer and such Conciliation Officer shall submit his findings within one month and if amicable settlement has been arrived at, the Tribunal shall pass an order to that effect. Explanation—For the purposes of this sub-section "Conciliation Officer" means any person or representative of an organisation referred to in Explanation to sub-section (/) of section 5 or the Maintenance Officers designated by the State Government under sub-section (/) of section 18 or any other person nominated by the Tribunal for this purpose.

7. **Constitution of Maintenance Tribunal**.—The State Government shall within a period of six months from the date of the commencement of this Act, by notification in Official Gazette, constitute for each Sub-division one or more Tribunals as may be specified in the notification for the purpose of adjudicating and deciding upon the order for maintenance under section 5.

(2) The Tribunal shall be presided over by an officer not below the rank of Sub- Divisional Officer of a State.

(3) Where two or more Tribunals are constituted for any area, the State Government may, by general or special order, regulate the distribution of business among them.

8. **Summary procedure in case of inquiry**.—In holding any inquiry under section 5, the Tribunal may, subject to any rules that may be prescribed by the State Government in this behalf, follow such summary procedure as it deems fit.

(2) The Tribunal shall have all the powers of a Civil Court for the purpose of taking evidence on oath and of enforcing the attendance of witnesses and of compelling the discovery and production of documents and

material objects and for such other purposes as may be prescribed; and the Tribunal shall be deemed to be a Civil Court for all the purposes of section 195 and Chapter XX VI of the Code of Criminal Procedure, 1973 (2 of 1974).

(3) Subject to any rule that may be made in this behalf, the Tribunal may, for the purpose of adjudicating and deciding upon any claim for maintenance, choose one or more persons possessing special knowledge of any matter relevant to the inquiry to assist it in holding the inquiry.

9. **Order for maintenance.**—If children or relatives, as the case may be, neglect or refuse to maintain a senior citizen being unable to maintain himself, the Tribunal may, on being satisfied of such neglect or refusal, order such children or relatives to make a monthly allowance at such monthly rate for the maintenance of such senior citizen, as the Tribunal may deem fit and to pay the same to such senior citizen as the Tribunal may, from time to time, direct.

(2) The maximum maintenance allowance which may be ordered by such Tribunal shall be such as may be prescribed by the State Government which shall not exceed ten thousand rupees per month.

10. **Alteration in allowance.**—(/) On proof of misrepresentation or mistake of fact or a change in the circumstances of any person, receiving a monthly allowance under section 9, for the maintenance ordered under that section to pay a monthly allowance for the maintenance, the Tribunal may make such alteration, as it thinks fit, in the allowance for the maintenance.

(2) Where it appears to the Tribunal that, in consequence of any decision of a competent Civil Court, any order made under section 9 should be cancelled or varied, it shall cancel the order or, as the case may be, vary the same accordingly.

11. **Enforcement of order of maintenance**—A copy of the order of maintenance and including the order regarding expenses of proceedings, as the case may be, shall be given without payment of any fee to the senior citizen or to parent, as the case may be, in whose favour it is made and such order may be enforced by any Tribunal in any place where the person against whom it is made, such Tribunal on being satisfied as to

the identity of the parties and the non-payment of the allowance, or as the case may be, expenses, due.

(2) A maintenance order made under this Act shall have the same force and effect as an order passed under Chapter IX of the Code of Criminal Procedure, 1973 (2 of 1974) and shall be executed in the manner prescribed for the execution of such order by that Code.

12. **Option regarding maintenance in certain cases.**— Notwithstanding anything contained in Chapter [X of the Code of Criminal Procedure 1973 (2 of 1974) where a senior citizen or a parent is entitled for maintenance under the said Chapter and also entitled for maintenance under this Act may, without prejudice to the provisions of Chapter [X of the said Code, claim such maintenance under either of those Acts but not under both.

13. **Deposit of maintenance amount.**—When an order is made under this Chapter, the children or relative who is required to pay any amount in terms of such order shall within thirty days of the date of announcing the order by the Tribunal, deposit the entire amount ordered in such manner as the Tribunal may direct.

14. **Award of interest where any claim is allowed**—Where any Tribunal makes an order for maintenance made under this Act, such Tribunal may direct that in addition to the amount of maintenance, simple interest shall also be paid at such rate and from such date not earlier than the date of making the application as may be determined by the Tribunal which shall not be less than five per cent. and not more than eighteen per cent.: Provided that where any application for maintenance under Chapter [IX of the Code of Criminal Procedure, 1973 (2 of 1974) is pending before a Court at the commencement of this Act, then the Court shall allow the withdrawal of such application on the request of the parent and such parent shall be entitled to file an application for maintenance before the Tribunal.

15. Constitution of Appellate Tribunal.—The State Government may, by notification in the Official Gazette, constitute one Appellate Tribunal for each district to hear the appeal against the order of the Tribunal.

(2) The Appellate Tribunal shall be presided over by an officer not below the rank of District Magistrate.

16. **Appeals**.—Any senior citizen or a parent, as the case may be, aggrieved by an order of a Tribunal may, within sixty days from the date of the order, prefer an appeal to the Appellate Tribunal: Provided that on appeal, the children or relative who is required to pay any amount in terms of such maintenance order shall continue to pay to such parent the amount so ordered, in the manner directed by the Appellate Tribunal: Provided further that the Appellate Tribunal may, entertain the appeal after the expiry of the said period of sixty days, if it is satisfied that the appellant was prevented by sufficient cause from preferring the appeal in time.

(2) On receipt of an appeal, the Appellate Tribunal shall, cause a notice to be served upon the respondent.

(3) The Appellate Tribunal may call for the record of proceedings from the Tribunal against whose order the appeal is preferred.

(4) The Appellate Tribunal may, after examining the appeal and the records called for either allow or reject the appeal.

(5) The Appellate Tribunal shall, adjudicate and decide upon the appeal filed against the order of the Tribunal and the order of the Appellate Tribunal shall be final: Provided that no appeal shall be rejected unless an opportunity has been given to both the parties of being heard in person or through a dully authorised representative.

(6) The Appellate Tribunal shall make an endeavour to pronounce its order in writing within one month of the receipt of an appeal.

(7) A copy of every order made under sub-section (5) shall be sent to both the parties free of cost.

17. **Right to legal representation**.—Notwithstanding anything contained in any law, no party to a proceeding before a Tribunal or Appellate Tribunal shall be represented by a legal practitioner.

18. **Maintenance Officer**.— The State Government shall designate the District Social Welfare or an officer not below the rank of a District Social Welfare Officer, by whatever name called as Maintenance Officer.

(2) The Maintenance Officer referred to in sub-section, shall represent a parent if he so desires, during the proceedings of the Tribunal, or the Appellate Tribunal, as the case may be.

CHAPTER III: ESTABLISHMENT OF OLDAGE HOMES

19. **Establishment of oldage homes**.—(/) The State Government may establish and maintain such number of oldage homes at accessible places, as it may deem necessary, in a phased manner, beginning with at least one in each district to accommodate in such homes a minimum of one hundred fifty senior citizens who are indigent.

(2)The State Government may, prescribe a scheme for management of old age homes, including the standards and various types of services to be provided by them which are necessary for medical care and means of entertainment to the inhabitants of such homes.

Explanation—For the purposes of this section, "indigent" means any senior citizen who is not having sufficient means, as determined by the State Government, from time to time, to maintain himself.

CHAPTER IV: PROVISIONS FOR MEDICAL CARE OF SENIOR CITIZEN

20. **Medical support for senior citizens**.—The State Government shall ensure that,—

(i) the Government hospitals or hospitals funded fully or partially by the Government shall provide beds for all senior citizens as far as possible;

(ii) separate queues be arranged for senior citizens;

(iii) facility for treatment of chronic, terminal and degenerative diseases is expanded for senior citizens;

(iv) research activities for chronic elderly diseases and ageing expanded;

(v) there are earmarked facilities for geriatric patients in every district hospital dully headed by a medical officer with experience in geriatric care.

CHAPTER V: PROTECTION OF LIFE AND PROPERTY OF SENIOR CITIZEN

21. **Measures for publicity, awareness, etc., for welfare of senior citizens**— —The State Government shall, take all measures to ensure that—

(i) the provisions of this Act are given wide publicity through public media including the television, radio and the print, at regular intervals;

(ii) the Central Government and State Government Officers, including the police officers and the members of the judicial service, are given periodic sensitization and awareness training on the issues relating to this Act;

(iii) effective co-ordination between the services provided by the concerned Ministries or Departments dealing with law, home affairs, health and welfare, to address the issues relating to the welfare of the senior citizens and periodical review of the same is conducted.

22. **Authorities who may be specified for implementing the provisions of this Act.**— The State Government may, confer such powers and impose such duties on a District Magistrate as may be necessary, to ensure that the provisions of this Act are properly carried out and the District Magistrate may specify the officer, subordinate to him, who shall exercise all or any of the powers, and perform all or any of the duties, so conferred or imposed and the local limits within which such powers or duties shall be carried out by the officer as may be prescribed.

(2) The State Government shall prescribe a comprehensive action plan for providing protection of life and property of senior citizens.

23. **Transfer of property to be void in certain circumstances.**— Where any senior citizen who, after the commencement of this Act, has transferred by way of gift or otherwise, his property, subject to the condition that the transferee shall provide the basic amenities and basic physical needs to the transferor and such transferee refuses or fails to provide such amenities and physical needs, the said transfer of property shall be deemed to have been made by fraud or coercion or under undue influence and shall at the option of the transferor be declared void by the Tribunal.

(2) Where any senior citizen has a right to receive maintenance out of an estate and such estate or part thereof is transferred, the right to receive maintenance may be enforced against the transferee if the transferee has notice of the right, or if the transfer is gratuitous; but not against the transferee for consideration and without notice of right.

(3) If, any senior citizen is incapable of enforcing the rights under sub-sections (/) and (2), action may be taken on his behalf by any of the organisation referred to in Explanation to sub-section (/) of section 5.

CHAPTER VI: OFFENCES AND PROCEDURE FOR TRIAL

24. Exposure and abandonment of senior citizen—Whoever, having the care or protection of senior citizen leaves, such senior citizen in any place with the intention of wholly abandoning such senior citizen, shall be punishable with imprisonment of either description for a term which may extend to three months or fine which may extend to five thousands rupees or with both.

25. Cognizance of offences.—Notwithstanding anything contained in the Code of Criminal Procedure, 1973 (2 of 1974), every offence under this Act shall be cognizable and bailable.

(2) An offence under this Act shall be tried summarily by a Magistrate.

CHAPTER VII: MISCELLANEOUS

26. Officers to be public servants.—Every officer or staff appointed to exercise functions under this Act shall be deemed to be a public servant within the meaning of section 21 of the Indian Penal Code(45 of 1860).

27. Jurisdiction of civil courts barred.—No Civil Court shall have jurisdiction in respect of any matter to which any provision of this Act applies and no injunction shall be granted by any Civil Court in respect of anything which is done or intended to be done by or under this Act.

28. Protection of action taken in good faith—No suit, prosecution or other legal proceeding shall lie against the Central Government, the State Governments or the local authority or any officer of the Government in respect of anything which is done in good faith or intended to be done in pursuance of this Act and any rules or orders made thereunder.

29. Power to remove difficulties.—If any difficulty arises in giving effect to the provisions of this Act, the State Government may, by order published in the Official Gazette, make such provisions not inconsistent with the provisions of this Act, as appear to it to be necessary or expedient for removing the difficulty: Provided that no such order shall be made after the expiry of a period of two years from the date of the commencement of this Act.

30. **Power of Central Government to give directions**——The Central Government may give directions to State Governments as to the carrying into execution of the provisions of this Act.

31. **Power of Central Government to review.**—The Central Government may make periodic review and monitor the progress of the implementation of the provisions of this Act by the State Governments.

32. **Power of State Government to make rules**—The State Government may, by notification in the Official Gazette, make rules for carrying out the purposes of this Act.

(2) Without prejudice to the generality of the foregoing power, such rules may provide for—

(a) the manner of holding inquiry under section 5 subject to such rules as may be prescribed under sub-section (/) of section 8;

(b) the power and procedure of the Tribunal for other purposes under subsection (2) of section 8;

(c) the maximum maintenance allowance which may be ordered by the Tribunal under sub-section (2) of section 9;

(d) the scheme for management of old age homes, including the standards and various types of services to be provided by them which are necessary for medical care and means of entertainment to the inhabitants of such homes under sub-section (2) of section 19;

(e) the powers and duties of the authorities for implementing the provisions of this Act, under sub-section (/) of section 22;111

(f) a comprehensive action plan for providing protection of life and property of senior citizens under sub-section (2) of section 22;

(g) any other matter which is to be, or may be, prescribed.

(3) Every rule made under this Act shall be laid, as soon as may be after it is made, before each House of State Legislature, where it consists of two Houses or where such legislature consists of one House, before that House.

About the authors

Siva Prasad Bose is a writer of introductory guidebooks on different aspects of Indian laws. He is also a retired electrical engineer, retired after many years of service in Uttar Pradesh Power Corporation Limited. He received his engineering degree from Jadavpur University, Kolkata and has a law degree from Meerut University, Meerut. His interests lie in the fields of family law, civil law, law of contracts, and any areas of law related to power electricity related issues.

Joy Bose is a software engineer and data scientist by profession.

Other books by Siva Prasad Bose

Introduction to Wills and Probate

Delays in Court Cases in India

Introduction to negotiable instruments

Introduction to marriage laws in India

Neighbor Problems in India and what to do about them

Managing Court Cases with Mental Strength

Introduction to Patents and Patent Law in India

Introduction to Property Law in India

www.ingramcontent.com/pod-product-compliance
Lightning Source LLC
Chambersburg PA
CBHW070419220526
45466CB00004B/1467